Dear Laurel [illegible]
   I so appre[ciate]
your work & hope
this book gives you
comfort & joy.

*[signature]*

D0392232

# DIY Rules for a WTF World

## How To Speak Up, Get Creative, and CHANGE THE WORLD

**KRISTA SUH**

GRAND CENTRAL PUBLISHING

New York  Boston

Copyright © 2018 by Krista Suh
Illustrations by Aurora Lady

Cover design by Claire Brown. Cover illustration by Aurora Lady. Cover copyright © 2018 by Hachette Book Group, Inc.

Hachette Book Group supports the right to free expression and the value of copyright. The purpose of copyright is to encourage writers and artists to produce the creative works that enrich our culture.

The scanning, uploading, and distribution of this book without permission is a theft of the author's intellectual property. If you would like permission to use material from the book (other than for review purposes), please contact permissions@hbgusa.com. Thank you for your support of the author's rights.

Grand Central Publishing
Hachette Book Group
1290 Avenue of the Americas, New York, NY 10104
grandcentralpublishing.com
twitter.com/grandcentralpub

First Edition: January 2018

Grand Central Publishing is a division of Hachette Book Group, Inc. The Grand Central Publishing name and logo is a trademark of Hachette Book Group, Inc.

The publisher is not responsible for websites (or their content) that are not owned by the publisher.

The Hachette Speakers Bureau provides a wide range of authors for speaking events. To find out more, go to www.hachettespeakersbureau.com or call (866) 376-6591.

Print book interior design by Ashley Prine, Tandem Books

Library of Congress Control Number: 2017951263

ISBNs: 978-1-5387-1233-7 (hardcover), 978-1-5387-1234-4 (ebook)

Printed in the United States of America

LSC-C

10  9  8  7  6  5  4  3  2  1

To all the wealthy handsome lovers who fund
my life of leisure, to George Soros for paying
me to protest, and to all the men
who open doors for me and expect an award.
This book is for you.

Just . . . kidding . . . this book is really for women.
This book is for the feminine in all of us,
women, men, or genderqueer. May we have
the courage to lift the haze.

# Contents

THEY HAD RED HATS ON . . . AND THEY THOUGHT THEY HAD TAKEN AMERICA BACK. WHAT THEY NEVER COUNTED ON WAS A MILLION WOMEN IN PINK HATS THAT ARE GOING TO TAKE AMERICA FORWARD.

—*Van Jones, political commentator and author*

Introduction: Lift the Haze

# INTRODUCTION
## Lift the Haze

On January 21, 2017, half a million women's rights supporters gathered in Washington, DC, enough of them wearing the now infamous "pussyhat" that they created a sea of pink. These handmade pink hats, knitted by women all over the country and all over the world, were spotted in great numbers at simultaneous marches across the globe. Total attendance at the marches was estimated between three and five million people—men and women—worldwide.

The pussyhat was on the cover of *Time* and the *New Yorker*, featured in countless political cartoons, and covered in publications all over the world. Jean Railla, quoted in the *New Yorker*, said the pussyhat is the "perfect symbol . . . It's both wholesome and sexual, handmade but shared through social media, brash enough for the meme era but also somehow incredibly sweet." Many writers, newscasters, and political commentators noted that the pussyhat became a successful symbol, despite early criticisms and mockery. The *New York Times* wrote "the handmade pink 'pussy hats' that marchers wore . . . had been sneered at in the days before the march. They were called corny, girlie, a waste of time. Seen from above, though, on thousands of marchers, their wave of color created a powerful image."

The pussyhat, the sea of pink, the symbol of resistance, the "greatest performance art piece of our time" (said by people who are not my mom) made a huge public statement. As the creator of the Pussyhat Project, I found myself overwhelmed in the days that followed the Women's March, beset by well-meaning ideas and opportunities from all sides. We could be a nonprofit, we could design hats for all marches and every cause, we could license the pussyhat and make a killing, we could send out daily or weekly calls to action to the resistance fighters, and so on.

All of these possibilities made sense, and I began to feel like following them was part of my duty. But my intuition was telling me otherwise. I didn't want to operate out of scarcity ("There's no time! You must capitalize on this moment NOW or it will go away!") and I didn't want to respond frenetically or reactively. The Pussyhat Project was designed to empower women, and after the Women's March, I needed to direct that empowering attention and care to myself.

The more I listened to my inner voice, the more I felt that the calls I was hearing from the nonprofit sector—the ones laser-focused on daily calls to action and consistently keeping the troops rallied—weren't really being directed at me. Knowledgeable, competent people were already doing this important work. They didn't need me.

I felt I was most needed in a scary and often dismissed place: the personal sphere, the realm of the innermost thoughts and feelings of women who feel crushed by the patriarchy, restricted by their lack of choice, and tortured by feelings of self-loathing. I didn't want to lead the charge in the way people wanted me to, even expected me to. Yes, the pussyhat made a big public splash and impressed reporters and attracted celebrated actors and thinkers and commentators and people prominent in the public sphere, but it also affected women's rights supporters personally.

"Thank you for giving me a way to channel my grief," many knitters told me. "I didn't know what to do with myself in the days after the election, and the Pussyhat Project was the first thing that was able to lift me out of my depression and give me the feeling I could do something." Knitting a pussyhat, contrary to its "frivolous" reputation, was an action that was deeply political and also deeply personal. We've all heard the slogan "the personal is political," first used in the women's movements of the 1960s and '70s. In our current movement, that sentiment is powerfully at play all over the country and the world.

My next step used the same blend of personal action for political change. I wanted to help women across the land be less afraid of speaking up. I wanted to help them to speak their minds, to live their best lives.

My instincts told me I should write a book—this book. I wasn't always a confident, pussyhat-wearing revolutionary. For too long I was afraid to speak up about what mattered to me and why. I was a writer in Los Angeles who was afraid to use Twitter because I was terrified of sharing myself and my opinions. I was a Hillary supporter who gave her my money and my time, but not my voice. I was too anxious to explain on social media exactly why I supported her campaign. And then she lost the election to Donald Trump, and something inside me snapped. I knew I couldn't let fear keep me from speaking up. I had so much to say, and I was ready to say it. I started writing a blog post and pressing "publish" every day for two weeks, until the Pussyhat Project launched, and that became an extension of everything I'd needed to say since the election.

After my experience with the Project's great success, I believe that there are two things that need to happen next, and simultaneously. We need to:

1. Reach out to the other side, so they can know us and we can know them, and together we can start caring about each other.
2. Urge people already on our side to be politically active.

I'm focused on the latter, and that's where this book comes in. In order for women to be politically active, they need to be confident in their abilities and confident in their bodies. To do that, we need to remove the patriarchal self-policing messages present in our minds (i.e., "squelchers"). I don't need a six-foot, four-inch white man to loom over me and tell me I'm stupid; I've already got that voice inside of me. How did that happen and how can I stop it? How can I learn to listen to my own voice and follow it? That is the guiding philosophy behind this book, and in it I will share how I learned to embody this confidence, and how you can too.

I know that this book isn't going to fit everyone's idea of the "right" kind of political activism. People have complained that "preaching to the choir" isn't the most efficient means of making change, but here's the thing: I know that reaching across the aisle is important, but I believe that the more urgent problem—the one I believe I am uniquely suited to address—is rooted in that very choir. "Don't preach to the choir," people say. But what if the choir is afraid to sing out? What if choir members are choking at the thought of speaking up, and what if the choir is persecuted, put down, or in fear for their lives? I think preaching to the choir is essential. How else can they sing?

If I can help more women find the confidence to speak up and get to know themselves and their opinions—and feel steadfast and stand by those opinions—then I believe I can create more change on a more meaningful plane, one that will have ripple effects we can only imagine. What if millions of women broke free of their fears and started saying what they truly thought, stating what they truly wanted, pursuing ideas that truly inspired them? We would have a revolution. If the success and scope of the Pussyhat Project has taught me anything, it's that we already have one. The idea of this book is to make that revolution even more far-reaching by starting on the deeply personal level.

Our personal journeys are important and exploring yours is essential preparation for living the life you want, essential maintenance for living your best life. Working on yourself *is* fundamental, and being the best *you* that you can be is only possible if you've got a solid grip on the fundamentals of who you are. That's why working on yourself is not fluffy or trivial or a waste of time. You are your own foundation. Every revolution starts with you.

People also say that focusing on the internal processes that keep us down isn't real activism. The fact is, all women are, in some sense, smothered by the patriarchy. Misogyny is like a haze; we can't touch it or even see it, but it's obscuring our vision, often without our realizing it. My hope is that this book will lift the haze so that women and girls from all walks of life can benefit together. I want this book to empower women to know themselves, and to put that knowledge into action. I want women to live their best lives.

After much soul-searching, this is my plan:

# Krista's Plan for World Illumination

1. Write this book to offer tips, opinions, and ideas on how to get rid of "idea squelchers" in our brains.
2. Inspire women to apply what works for them in their lives on a practical level, maybe even daily.
3. Start a movement for women and girls to be more fearless in their lives, to speak up, and to pursue their ideas and dreams— maybe the next Pussyhat Project, or a run for president of the United States, or a nonprofit that addresses and solves starvation, or any project or task that enables them to create a path toward change.
4. And inspire world peace, because why not think big? Why not imagine the best-case scenario?

That's my why, and this book is the how.

\* \* \*

You can read this book any way you want to. Front to back, back to front. You can flip to any page in the book and see what randomly comes up. Like a Magic 8-Ball, you can shake the book and see what chapter serves up the answer to your current questions.

The chapters are short and you can read one or all of them in whatever time you have—maybe you're riding the subway to work or you're in the car waiting in the pickup line at your children's elementary school, maybe you are going to bed and want one last idea for your brain to play with before you go to sleep, or maybe you're taking the day off and reading the book in one passionate swoop at a bohemian café—*all ways are valid.*

This book has two different types of chapters. The first is more philosophical, like a bedtime story or a Zen koan you can read and let settle into your mind. The second is more action-oriented, accompanied by an exercise. You can read the chapter and do the exercise right away, no matter where you are. If you're in the mood for an activity, flip through the book and look for the boxed exercises.

The first six chapters are what I refer to as my "toolkit," my core set of fundamental helpful rules and beliefs that the rest of the chapters are in some way based on.

1. *The Bellows: Everything changes. You'll need different rules at different times.*

2. *The Pharmacy: You can choose what rules to prescribe yourself.*

3. *Intuition: Use your intuition to decide what rule you need to prescribe.*

4. *The Science Fair: Treat the process of rule selection like a science experiment. You're allowed to make mistakes.*

5. *The Valid Stamp: You choose what is valid. There is no official "right" way to do things.*

6. *Training Wheels: Treat yourself like a child, a beginner. Don't dismiss helpful tools just because they seem baby-ish or you think you ought to know better.*

When I first started the Pussyhat Project, I didn't know what was going to happen. I used these ideas to get the project started, and a movement began.

Whatever you want to do in your life, I hope this book helps you do it, with passion, gusto, purpose, and joy.

XO,

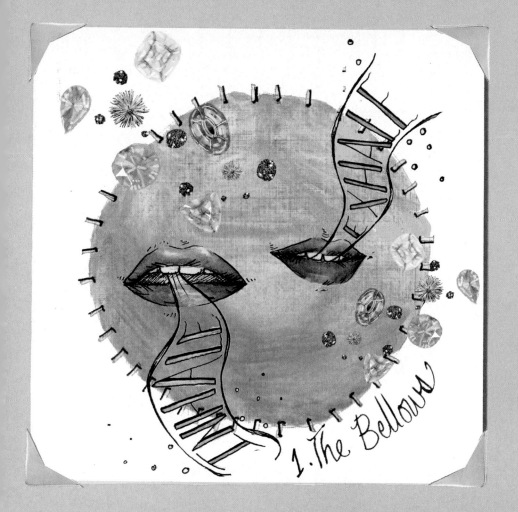

1. The Bellow

# CHAPTER 1
# The Bellows

I'd pat myself on the back for coming up with such a nifty idea as "The Bellows," but it's actually the main point of the oldest book of wisdom on record—the *I Ching*—which boils down to one message: everything changes.

Fire bellows look kind of like an accordion: when you expand them, they suck in lots of air, and when you contract them, they blow out a lot of air into the fire, feeding the flames with oxygen. Creativity is like the fire, and the bellows is your tool to keep the fire going. There are times when you will need to expand and inhale every experience you can, developing and strengthening yourself. And then there are times when you will need to contract and exhale every experience, producing and creating with every breath until you are empty again. And then the process repeats.

Human beings are not static. When we inhale and take in experiences, we're saying *yes* to opportunities, but in doing so, we have a tendency to be hard on ourselves: *Why am I not focused on one project? Why am I scattered everywhere? Why can't I get my life together? Why do I not know what I want?* You are in an inhaling and expanding stage—you are exploring your options, you are seeing what's out there!

And yet, when we go into an exhaling stage—constricting, homing in on the thing we're trying to create—our thought pattern unhelpfully changes to, *Why am I so limited? Why am I not doing lots of exciting things like my colleagues? Why am I so boring? I've said no or want to say no to all these invitations, and now I have a fear of missing out.* This is your time of intense focus, and there's value and benefit in this action as well—it's simply different from the action of inhaling.

A lot of times, our discomfort in life comes from either 1) needlessly questioning the stage of life we are in, or 2) staying in a stage too long out of fear of change.

If we can just acknowledge that the stages of our lives ebb and flow, and that we have about as much control as we do over the tides, we can troubleshoot our lives and much more quickly get out of the doldrums. Next time you feel stressed, a good question to ask is yourself is this: Are you inhaling or exhaling right now? And whichever stage you are in, can you accept that, or is it time to change it up?

I think of the song "Turn! Turn! Turn!" by the Byrds, and the fact that there truly is a time and a season for everything. This includes all of your goals and passions, because whatever you want in life involves engaging with the creative process. The inhaling phase is a critical exploratory phase of this process. Exhaling is the execution part of the creative process. Both are absolutely necessary, but while the execution phase is lauded, the exploratory phase is mocked.

The summer of 2016 was an inhaling period for me, in which I explored lots of things, including knitting. At the time, a lot of my relatives judged me because it appeared that I wasn't working or doing anything significant. But this period was significant and fruitful. Had I not spent that time inhaling, I would not have been able to exhale the Pussyhat Project in the fall. One of the biggest false assumptions we let ourselves be guided by is that we are consistent beings. It's not true. We are constantly changing, constantly in flux. The trick is being aware of these movements, and leaning into them.

If you want to amp up your creativity and have a bigger impact on the world, understanding your own rhythms will be a big help. Get to know your rhythms, accept your rhythms (i.e., don't assume your rhythms are worse than someone else's!), embrace your rhythms, and then leverage your rhythms so you can be the best instrument you can to implement change in the world.

It's kind of like when you go shopping: a big "aha!" moment for women is when they realize it's up to the dress to suit the body, not the body to suit the dress. You want the schedule you "put on" to suit your natural rhythms, not the other way around. The expectations you have for yourself—about when you can produce good work and when you can breathe in and explore—need to match your unique natural rhythms, not some imaginary rubric of when it's "acceptable" to do something.

Personally, it took me about ten years to understand the rhythms of my body and mind, and I think if I had removed guilt from the process, it could have taken me less than a year.

For example, if I simply noted and accepted I was in an inhale stage rather than beating myself up over being so unfocused, I might have made progress and met my goals more quickly.

I work kind of like a lioness, who sleeps fifteen to eighteen hours a day. When she's awake, she hunts and takes care of cubs. It's pretty embarrassing to admit that, because that means in a given year, I could spend 75 percent of it "sleeping"—relaxing exploring, inhaling—and only 25 percent on "output"—creating, earning, helping, exhaling. It's why I like to work in sprints. I like to concentrate my time and effort and energy into one burst of exuberant hunting.

An inhale period for me could look like:
- Taking knitting and crochet classes at The Little Knittery
- Exploring new restaurants
- Taking a contortion class

- Going to the beach at midnight
- Meeting new people at mixers
- Reading YA fantasy novels

An exhale period for me could look like:
- Working on the Pussyhat Project
- Writing a screenplay
- Writing this book

Inhaling and exhaling isn't just something that individuals do. This is a concept that (broadly) applies to grand-scale societal changes as well as personal life shifts. I find it especially useful when applied to teamwork.

When leading or working in a team, it's helpful to note who is in inhale mode and who is in exhale mode. It's also helpful as the leader to express what stage you are in and what expectations you have of the group—inhale or exhale? This helps calibrate as best you can the different stages of the team members in order to produce the result you want. An intern might be in inhale mode, and they simply want to experience all they can in the job. An artist might be in exhale mode, and they will approach the task by saying, "Give me the specs, I am raring to go, let's put this vision together." And remember, not only is each person a living organism, but *the team itself* is a living organism that is not going to stay consistent. When it works, it really works. You know when you are part of a group project and it feels great and everything just clicks? It's probably because all of you are in "fuck yeah" exhale mode *at the same time*.

The trick to using The Bellows to your advantage is being willing to accept that forcing yourself into a stage you just aren't in will only frustrate you. Your rhythms aren't something you can will into being different. Accepting this about yourself, and learning to watch your own personal tide, will go a long way toward healing your broken expectations of yourself. So, are you inhaling or exhaling?

Remember, as the *I Ching* tells us, everything changes.

2. The Pharmacy

# CHAPTER 2
# The Pharmacy

*The second most basic rule I use is called The Pharmacy.*
Since we are not consistent beings (The Bellows), what we need to "prescribe" ourselves is constantly changing.

Statements of conventional wisdom don't work for every experience. Instead, you have to cultivate the awareness to prescribe them when and where they are actually needed. For example, let's take two different aphorisms:

1. *Pull yourself up by the bootstraps! (Cousin of "No pain, no gain!" and "Power through it!")*
2. *Know when to quit.*

If I'm trying my darnedest at something and it's just not working, and I've worked myself to the bone, I might need to prescribe aphorism #2. But if I'm dragging my feet about something because, although I want to do it, I'm afraid of failing and what other people might think, then I need to prescribe myself aphorism #1. There will be times when #1 is "true" and "right" or when #2 is "true" and "right." Similarly, it's worth noting that what works for someone else might not work for you.

The most important takeaway here is that it's up to *you* to discern what is needed most in every situation. You are the pharmacist. You are the boss.

Speaking of that:

1. Listen to the advice of your elders, learn from their mistakes.
2. Listen to yourself, trust yourself.

It's up to you to decide when to try someone else's way and when to try your own. But remember: ultimately, it is still up to you! A woman's right to choose goes so much further than reproductive rights; it's also her right to choose how she frames her unique experiences and her own thoughts.

Because this is something we so often forget, we need reminders. So here is a friendly reminder for you: you prescribe your own thoughts.

3. Intuition

# CHAPTER 3
## *Intuition*

*How do you know when your life needs to change? How* do you know when one good idea fits your situation or when it doesn't? Should you go faster and urge yourself to "go for it," or should you slow down and encourage yourself to "stop to smell the roses"? The answer is: use your intuition.

Your intuition will guide you and show you what thoughts will best serve you in any given moment.

Intuition as a concept is often maligned. There is a famous study in which researchers interviewed workers at a chick sorting facility.[1] Cute, fuzzy, yellow baby chicks slide down a gently sloped metal chute where they must be sorted into male and female groups. There is no machine able to sort them this way, so human beings are used to determine the sex. At first the workers pick up each chick individually to examine their genitalia to see whether it is male or female. But after a while, every worker is able to sort the chick by sex without picking it up; in fact, they can tell from yards away if a chick is male or female, and their determination (aka intuition)

1  Richard Horsey, "The Art of Chicken Sexing," *UCL Working Papers in Linguistics* 14 (2002), 107–17.

is close to 100 percent correct. When scientists asked them how they knew the correct answer, none of the workers had an explanation. They could just *tell*. They just *knew*. That's a prime example of intuition.

We do all kinds of things every day without thinking about it. For example, if you reach for a glass right now, you probably won't notice that your hands automatically shape into a curve. That's your body, your intuition, helping you to be more effective in the world, without having to be asked.

Your intuition resides in your body. I love Regena Thomashauer's works, *Mama Gena's School of Womanly Arts* and *Pussy*. She uses the word "pussy" as shorthand for feminine intuition as well as the part of a woman's body that includes her vagina, vulva, and clitoris. When I created the pussyhat, "pussy" was a handy reference to counteract Trump's deplorable comments, but I also loved that using the word "pussy" was a reclamation of feminine intuition, something that has been much maligned in our culture, probably because it is so powerful. When women embrace intuition, they can change the world.

The more we remove the patriarchal voices in our heads, the more we can hear our intuition speak its truth. When we act on our intuition, we make decisions quickly and we move through the world confidently and with purpose and joy, and isn't that how we'd all like to live?

At the beginning of my journey, it was difficult to ascertain which voice in my head belonged to my intuition. I wish I could go back to that younger me and tell her that the intuitive voice is *never* the one that speaks out of fear. Any fear-driven voice is not your intuition. Your worries are not your intuition. Sometimes the fears and worries do point you toward something that is wrong or needs attention, but the intuitive voice itself is not fearful. If you're in a bad situation and need to run, your fearful voices will scream, *RUN! GODDAMNIT, RUN!!* But your intuitive voice will just say, "Run. Now." It will be calm and firm, and it will not pitch you into freak-out mode. Sometimes the intuitive voice may sound urgent, but it's only because we have ignored it for so long that fears and worries come in to hype it up.

Trust your intuition. Let it guide you. It won't push you around like all of those "shoulds" the patriarchy insists upon and would have you listen to over your own internal voice.

## The Midas Touch

So how do we get in touch with our intuition? Our feelings? Our bodies? I remember reading various self-help books in which the authors suggested noting where in my body I was feeling a feeling, and I felt completely lost. Was this confusion located . . . in my shoulder? In my chest? In my neck? My thighs? Years later, I did "get" what this meant—and now I can feel where I carry stress, where I hold worry, etc.—but I can never forget how annoyed I was by my difficulties with the exercise. I just couldn't get in touch with what I was feeling in my own body.

In my own fumbling journey, I invented an exercise I love called "The Midas Touch Journal." It's perfect for beginners like me. If you don't count yourself as someone in touch with her body or with her feelings, then start very literally. What are you *feeling*, with your hands, every day?

This exercise is great for getting in touch with your body, and as a useful (and fun!) side effect, it's a way to focus on creating an environment that *feels* good to you instead of one that just looks good to other people. By focusing on the feeling, you'll end up with a space that nurtures you instead of a poor imitation of whatever happens to be trending in this month's *Architectural Digest*. You have the power to make your environment into something that supports and nourishes your awareness of the world and your intuition. Don't give that up just for the sake of what's fashionable or expected of you.

The best part about the Midas Touch Journal is that it reminds you to value what feels good to you, not what looks good to others. You might like how something looks, and another person might disagree, and you might then question your opinion. What looks good is debatable, and we often forget how very individual visual taste is. But touch is so inherently personal

EXERCISE

# The Midas Touch Journal

For one day, from the moment you wake up to the moment you go to sleep, make a list of EVERY item you touch.

| | |
|---|---|
| 1. Sheets, mattress, bed | 6. Carpet |
| 2. Pillowcase, pillow | 7. Toothbrush |
| 3. Notebook | 8. Toothpaste |
| 4. Pen | 9. Sink faucet handle |
| 5. Mug, water | And so on . . . Be as detailed as you can. |

At the end of the day, look over your list (it might be well over one hundred items long) and circle areas that didn't feel good to you. Note why, and write down what you can do to fix this area so it feels good next time. It's not just how it feels on your skin; it's how it makes you feel.

For example: For years, I slept on super scratchy sheets I disliked, but I didn't address it until I did the Midas Touch Journal and realized I needed to take action. Yes, it was a small part of my conscious waking life, but that little surge of unpleasantness was unnecessary; it repeated every day and every night, and it was totally fixable. I replaced the sheets with new sheets I love and now when I wake up or snuggle in for the night, it's a moment not of unpleasantness, not of neutrality, but of *joy*. The Midas Touch Journal is also a great way to address the flow of your living situation. Perhaps, like me, if you want to wake up to a mug of water and a notebook and pen, you might want to *put* a mug of water and a notebook and pen on a nightstand next to the bed. It's not rocket science, but it's amazing how we can allow these little unpleasant moments to go on for years.

By studying your Midas Touch Journal, you can turn every touch interaction you have into sensory gold.

that two people literally can't touch the same spot at the same time and have the exact same experience. If something *feels* good to you as you run your fingers through it, you don't really care if other people agree, because you can't possibly expect them to feel what you're feeling, and you don't care if they don't feel the same way. Intuition is like that; it *is* that. Intuition takes place in your body and doesn't need an overt thumbs-up. If it feels good to you, that is your intuition speaking.

---

**EXERCISE**

## 5-Sensation Snapshot

Eyes: What is delighting your sense of sight right now?

Ears: What is delighting your sense of hearing right now?

Nose: What is delighting your sense of smell right now?

Mouth: What is delighting your sense of taste right now?

Fingers: What is delighting your sense of touch right now?

When you feel restless and don't know what your next move is, you can ask yourself these questions to ground yourself in the here and now. You can do this exercise several times in a week and the answers may vary wildly! It's a great way to get in touch with your body, using all the senses instead of just sight.

---

# The Point of Resonance

res·o·nance \rez-uh-nuh ns\ noun: resonance; plural noun: resonances

**1.** The quality in a sound of being deep, full, and reverberating.
*"the resonance of his voice"*

**1.1.** The power to evoke enduring images, memories, and emotions.
*"the concepts lose their emotional resonance"*

One afternoon my singer-songwriter friend Connie (aka MILCK) and I were taking a walk through my downtown L.A. neighborhood. We were at the Walt Disney Concert Hall—that curved, metallic rose of a building—and like a kid with a secret playground, I urged her to follow me up the stairs to a little-known garden. During intermission, concertgoers can come out to this garden, stretch their legs, maybe smoke. But the rest of the time, anyone can go up and enjoy the fountain and the flowering trees and plants. There is also a Children's Amphitheatre, with free performances throughout the year, and I wanted to show Connie this little outdoor stage. My friend brightened as she saw the space, recognizing it from one of her previous performances. All of a sudden, I was no longer the tour guide. Instead, she was the expert as she ran around the shell of the amphitheater. She was so excited to show me something, and walked around humming and singing until she found it—the point of resonance. It was the sweet spot in the theater where if you stood at a certain point on the stage and spoke, it would reverberate through your body and your voice would amplify to the audience without the need for a microphone.

"Come here," she urged. "Can you feel it?" I was too shy at the time to sing out, even in front of my good friend.

Later, I returned to the Children's Amphitheatre alone and tried to find that point of resonance. I was singing in the dark, walking around the stage and feeling like a fool, but also feeling kind of naughty and mischievous in a delicious way. Eventually, I found that point. I didn't really believe it would be so obvious, but it was. I felt it *immediately*. I felt vibrations. I could hear that my voice was louder even though I put no extra effort into it.

This is what intuition is like, what it feels like. You kind of fumble around alone in the dark, or in front of amused onlookers, trying different spots, trying again, moving around, continuing to sing, until you *feel it*. You find resonance. You find "the right answer" because it resonates in your body. Nobody has to tell you what you know, because you already know it.

We are taught how to solve problems or find solutions in a very different way. For example, we're told that if you think about something long enough, you can find the right answer and skip the loser-ish part of wandering around looking like an idiot. But just using the intellect and ignoring what our intuition tells us can actually take longer.

Let's just say that instead of wandering around and using my intuition to feel the space, I decide to sit at the back of the amphitheater to study its curves, to note the wind changes, and to study other people wandering around. Finally, after much analysis, when I think I have my point selected, I go down, open my mouth, and *sing*, hoping that I have skipped the fumbling-around-looking-silly part and have found the point of resonance on my first try. The problem with this "face-saving" method is that after a few seconds, I'll stop singing and ask the audience, "Uh, is this working? Is this resonating?" You'll get mixed messages from the audience, and it will feel like criticism and you won't get the answers you want. Even if people say, "You're great!" you might question them because you haven't had the journey of finding resonance. You haven't felt non-resonance and resonance, so you're unsure about the difference. But once you go on that experimental journey, singing in different spots, you'll feel the resonance in yourself in your body. This is the beauty of trusting your intuition.

When you find the courage to just let go of the fear of what other people think of you while you're wandering the stage (experimenting, trying new things), you will find the resonance point in your body, and then you won't *care* what other people think because you will know, without a doubt, that it feels right and is right for you.

This applies to most things, including developing a personal style that's right for you. When it comes to style, it's tempting to look for someone to just tell you what works for you and what doesn't (hello, fashion magazines). And while you can find inspiration in magazines, they can't simply hand you your resonance point in fashion; you have to find it and *feel* it yourself. And that means putting on different clothes and seeing if they *feel* right. And then walking out into the world in this outfit and seeing if that feels right. The more you do this, the more you hone in on your individual resonance point. At times it will change and you won't feel the resonance in an outfit anymore, and you wander a bit, putting on different clothes and seeing how they feel, and find the resonance point again.

---

### EXERCISE

## "Ugly" Fashion

*Find the ugliest piece of clothing you can pull off—that's style.*

Find the "ugliest" piece of fashion you can find that works for you. Look in your closet, perhaps in the hand-me-downs, find a piece, and build an outfit around that.

Or, next time you go shopping, find the "ugliest" piece of clothing in each store and try it on to see if anything surprises you.

When we play with what we deem "ugly" we might find a surprising creative combination that resonates.

Often we forget that we have the agency to decide what is right for ourselves. Instead we hand that decision over to others, feeling embarrassed when other people judge us (Who wore it better? Hot or not? Do or don't?), when really, it's all about whether or not you're feeling the vibration in yourself. When you know it's working for *you*, it doesn't matter what other people think.

4. The Science Fair

# CHAPTER 4
# The Science Fair

Were you ever in a science fair as a kid? Remember the tables set up in the gym? The poster boards you made displaying your findings? Did you spring for the triptych board—the poster board with three sides to it?

Too often, we treat every new experience in our lives as a life-or-death, make-or-break situation, when really it's more of a kid's science fair. You are your own science experiment. As we explore, we are making our own poster boards that showcase our findings. And the results of the experiment aren't "good" or "bad"—they're just more information to work with.

Because everything is always changing (remember we are not static beings, and our likes and dislikes, even our surroundings, are constantly in flux), rather than choosing a New Year's resolution every year to incorporate for *the rest of your life*, I'd recommend choosing one to two things you want to explore in a science experiment for the next six to eight weeks.

For example, perhaps you think you need to be more structured with your time and get more sleep. For the next six to eight weeks, go to bed at 11:30 p.m. and see if the results benefit you. If it causes more trouble than it's worth, then stop doing it after the experiment is over. But if it is helpful to your life, and you find yourself being less snappish to your family in the morning (or to your boss or your dog or your kid), you can decide to keep this habit for as long as you see fit. Because within the six to eight weeks of the experiment, it probably will become a habit.

You might want to try the opposite experiment—perhaps you want to be less structured in your schedule and want more time to play and be creative. For six to eight weeks you can schedule nothing outside of work, or if you're able, schedule no work and see what you are like and what you create when you have no agenda. While this might seem like a lot, six to eight weeks is not a big chunk of your life, and the findings you get from the experiment are invaluable to enriching the rest of your life.

Here are some experiments you can try:

- Don't eat refined sugar (I've never tried this, but I hear it's great).
- Floss every day.
- Wear sunscreen every day.
- Say one nice thing to your significant other every day.
- Write down three things you're grateful for every night.
- Take a bubble bath every two weeks.
- Read a book by a woman and/or person of color every week. I call this my 100 WOC + POC Author Project, and have made bookplates to chart my progress. (You can download them for free on my website kristasuh.com.)
- Meditate every morning. Start with seven minutes and work up from there.

What science experiment would you like to conduct on yourself for six to eight weeks?

## Triptych

Buy a cardboard triptych, the kind kids use at science fairs, and then present your experiment on the triptych like you're a science project at the fourth grade science fair. It's a fun, silly, tactile reminder that all of your self-improvement projects are just exploratory experiments, and you can collect the results as helpful data points, not things to feel bad or ashamed about. In fact, in the spirit of playfulness (which is a component of both experiments AND science), I highly encourage glitter on the triptych.

You can make one on your own or you can invite your friends over to make your own science fair. Have everyone make and decorate a triptych and then go around presenting your findings to your fellow scientists. What are you exploring now? What are you hoping to find out about yourself? How's it going? Any results so far that have made you realize something about yourself? Have you adjusted your process? What will your next science experiment be?

5. The Valid Stamp

# CHAPTER 5
# The Valid Stamp

The patriarchy's greatest victory is to suggest—through peer pressure, social convention, or other means—that there is only one right way of doing something, and that your way (particularly if you are a woman) is wrong. When I am getting nervous about accomplishing a task or doing a job, concerned about the *way* I'm getting it done, I have to remind myself that it's a lie to say there is only one right way of doing what I'm trying to do. Our patriarchal society has conditioned us to believe that the way approved by the powers that be is the only way.

For example, I wanted to pay someone a certain way, with this easy, breezy app, but I was like, *No, I have to go to a bank, get more checks, and write a check because that is more professional*, and then I had to stop and ask why I was thinking about that, when the way I'd already decided upon was the most effective and convenient for me. I ended up paying with my easy, breezy app, and of course it was fine. But take that small, benign example and magnify that into EVERY DAMN SECOND OF OUR LIVES and it's no wonder we're so exhausted. It requires an enormous amount of energy to question the way you choose to do everything in your life, from the most mundane tasks to the most profound.

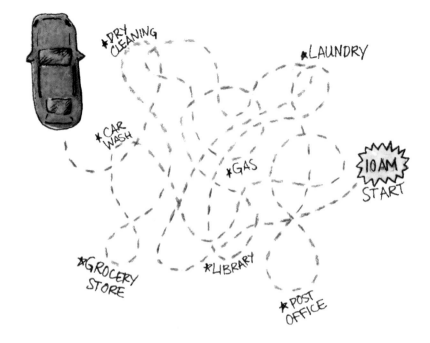

What if you, and you alone, were the arbiter of what is valid? What if you could decide what was the best way to do even the littlest things? For instance, are you the sort of person who goes out to do errands and tries to maximize your time, doing it quickly while saving gas, never paying for parking, etc.? What if you just did the errands in the order you felt like doing them? What if doing errands in a non-efficient way—even doing a little bit of dawdling and window-shopping along the way—is perfectly valid?

Just like the guiding principle of The Pharmacy (15), the prescription that works for some people might not work for others. Perhaps you do want and need help to get ahold of your schedule in order to maximize your time. Fine; there are amazing resources out there for you, and I hope you're not ashamed to look into that. Or maybe you have fallen under the spell that maximizing your schedule is the valid, "right" way of doing things. What if it isn't? Imagine how that might change your life for the better!

I like to imagine that EVERYONE gets a "valid" stamp where you can validate anything in your life. You can validate yourself, you can validate your emotions, you can validate your decisions. You need not seek someone else's "valid" stamp or the patriarchy's "valid" stamp. You can if you want to, for fun, but it's optional, because you get to determine what is stamped valid or not with *your* stamp in *your* life.

---

EXERCISE

## Make Your Own Valid Stamp

Write "VALID" in big letters on top of every page of your journal.

If you want to get crafty, you can take a potato and carve out "VALID" backward into it, and then have fun stamping it in paint on a piece of paper. The *feeling* you will get from pressing that "valid" stamp onto paper will cement the feeling of joy—it will be a physical reminder that yes, indeed, you are the arbiter of what is valid in your life. The tactile physical ritual of actually stamping "VALID" onto something is itself a form of magic.

---

6. Training Wheels

# CHAPTER 6
# Training Wheels

When trying out a new thought or rule, it's important to remember that "NEW" is the operative word. It's a mistake to expect ourselves to be awesome and expert at anything when we're at the beginning of our learning process, when we're just starting out. It's also a mistake to be embarrassed by the idea of being a beginner. I've seen so many kids freak out over training wheels on a bicycle—they don't want to be "babyish" in front of the other kids. Looking back, I wish I had kept my training wheels on longer because learning how to ride a bike was one of the most traumatic experiences of my childhood, and it didn't have to be. I learned without training wheels in a crowded garage around a ping-pong table with sharp corners, so if I fell I'd instantly get scraped. I wish I could go back and encourage the adult in charge to take me somewhere else—why make it so hard?

But a resistance to so-called "babyish" training wheels follows us into adulthood. Just as a kid might scoff at training wheels ("Ugh, training wheels are for *babies*, and I'm not a baby"), we adults might look at a helpful online course, self-help book, life coach, or therapist and scoff, "Ugh, those things are for losers/hippies/failures/weirdos and I'm not a loser/hippie/failure/weirdo."

Whenever you have a strong reaction to something that is meant to help you, I would encourage you to stop a moment and see if you can give it a try, even a small brief try. Do an intro session with a therapist, try the online course, buy the book. If you can learn NOT to be afraid of being embarrassed as you're learning something new, you will really have nothing to lose. Sure, you might be out a few bucks if you buy a book that is unhelpful to you or a course that isn't a good fit for you, but in the long run, you've gained knowledge about yourself and what works for you and what doesn't. It's all an investment in yourself. For most people, it's not the money that scares them about putting on a set of training wheels, it's the shame.

If we can lose the shame, we can learn all sorts of things and become stronger people. It's a Darwinian advantage to use training wheels. The most engaging and fascinating people are the ones who are constantly trying new things, people who are willing to be a beginner all the time, again and again.

I have to constantly remind myself to treat myself like a kid—if you were raising a child, you would want her or him to have all the tools necessary to learn in a fun, efficient, and (hopefully) stress-free way. Beginners and kids actually need MORE tools, so it's good to invest in yourself in that way. It's a mistake to expect yourself to be a master right away. You'll only get discouraged and give up before you've gotten the chance to find what might be a real source of pleasure.

For example, if you're just learning how to cook, why start with the hardest recipe? And why start with a hard recipe AND not have the correct tools and the best ingredients to make it? Having fresh ingredients and great spices is so amazing for a beginner chef because you are setting yourself up to succeed. The beginner needs and deserves these great ingredients, whereas the advanced chef can actually "make do" with crap ingredients and make something amazing out of them. I hear a lot of people saying, "No, I won't buy that tool for myself until I'm better at it," but really, the time you need the tool the most is probably right now, when you're a beginner. Expert chefs don't need the tools as much (although they are very picky about knives).

When you're not afraid of being a beginner or playing the fool, you occupy a place of power, and you have the potential to make great advances. I constantly have to remind myself that it's okay to put on training wheels and look awkward while I learn. It's not only okay to mess up, it's part of the process. Practice imperfection, in other words.

It's also amazing to design a process to be as easy for yourself as possible—to streamline it, so to speak—so that you can save your grit and willpower for things that you really care about. If I hadn't shifted my focus away from being perfect at the very beginning of something new, I would never have done the Pussyhat Project. I would have allowed perfectionism to get in my own way. So, no shame, put on the training wheels!

7. All the Flowers are in the Bathroom: Creating Impact

# CHAPTER 7

# All the Flowers Are in the Bathroom: Creating Impact

I threw my twenty-sixth birthday party in my apartment. I bought some flowers from the downtown wholesale market in Los Angeles, maybe seven arrangements or so, a mix of daisies, lilies, and roses. I could have put them all over the apartment, e.g., one arrangement in the living room, one at the entrance, one in the kitchen, etc. Instead, I put all seven arrangements in the tiny bathroom. They crowded the whole counter, leaving just enough room for the sink and a bar of soap. Reflected in the bathroom mirror, all the flowers resembled a floral jungle.

Throughout the night, as people visited the bathroom, they would find me afterward and say, "Wow, you have a lot of flowers." The flowers were noticed. They looked beautiful, and they made an impact on guests. Had they been scattered all around the apartment, I would have needed maybe five times the amount of flowers in order to make the same impact.

You can apply this example of party floral arrangement to your life. If you want to make an impact, and I'm sure you do, pick a point to focus your energies on and go big on that one element. It will be noticed, and thus appreciated. It's not that my guests are begrudging people who can't appreciate flowers; it's that they can't appreciate them if the flowers aren't noticed at all. Concentrate the focus. Like I did with flowers in the bathroom, choose your area of focus. Don't automatically direct your energies to places you're told are the "right" or "appropriate" ones.

For the Pussyhat Project, while we welcomed people to make hats for their hometown sister march, we put all our core efforts into getting hats to the Women's March on Washington, DC, in order to make the most impact. At the March, we would GO BIG. I picked a very specific thing to throw my energies into, a detail really. And the hats literally topped off the march. I encourage you to see what happens when you throw your weight behind one detail and let the rest be, even for a day or a week. Even for a single hour.

## Red Sea Blue Ocean

Red Sea Blue Ocean is a business concept in which the red sea is where all your competitors are duking it out and the water becomes bloody. Blue ocean is where you want to be—a place no one else occupies. So if you direct your energies toward the blue ocean, and concentrate your focus in that neglected place, you will create big impact. Similarly, when you're being creative, it's best to focus your efforts in the areas nobody else has discovered. Not only do you avoid competition, but you are focusing on an area that *needs* you and your ideas. There were already geniuses at work doing the planning of the march, so how could I use my skills in an area that needed some magic? That's part of how the Pussyhat Project was born.

You don't need to just do the literal opposite of what other people are doing. Instead, I recommend you find places where you are already sticking out and thinking differently, and rather than berating yourself for being weird, see it as an opportunity to be in the blue ocean and make a big impact.

EXERCISE

## Overlooked Details

Next time you are asked to help out on a group project, encourage yourself to volunteer for a small, overlooked detail.

For example, if you're asked to take part in a bake sale, rather than signing up to watch the booth or bake cookies, say you'll be in charge of napkins. Just that. Napkins. What can you do to make napkins steal the show? What napkins will make people remember this bake sale? What napkins will make this bake sale the talk of the town?

Here are some of my brainstormed ideas:

Engraved napkins

Napkins with inspirational quotes on them

Rainbow colored napkins

Napkins folded into origami shapes

Napkins arranged in a mosaic

Napkins arranged into a pixelated picture of Hillary Clinton

Napkin dispenser that talks every time you pull one out

Napkins printed with a call to action

Napkins rolled into a keepsake napkin ring

Now you try. What type of napkins would transform this bake sale?

1.

2.

3.

4.

5.

If not napkins, what is another overlooked detail of the bake sale you could take on?

1.

2.

3.

Think about the products you love. Is there a detail they focus on that they direct extra attention to? For example, Yogi tea has an inspirational quote on every tea bag. Tiffany's offers those iconic blue boxes that are almost as coveted as what's inside. Ted Baker clothing has mischievous little labels with jokes on them sewn into their clothes. When you unzip your Lucky jeans, you read a message about how lucky you are.

Think about where in your pantry or closet at home a detail is celebrated. Write down the product and the detail.

1.

2.

3.

Think about where in your closet of clothes a detail is celebrated. Write down the product and the detail.

1.

2.

3.

Can you list any other examples where you see a detail being celebrated and making an impact you appreciate?

1.

2.

3.

If you've never witnessed your own power to make an impact, it's because you've never directed your energy at a single point. Try it and see what happens.

8. You Can Skin a Deer

# CHAPTER 8
# You Can Skin a Deer

*I'm a city girl, and my aunt is always telling me stories* about her childhood on the farm and how she plucked her own chickens. It's true; she can pluck a chicken, and I cannot.

One day my aunt and I were catching up and she mentioned that her son, my cousin, was volunteering at a wolf preservation center and one of his duties was skinning deer.

Purely to taunt her, I said, "Aunt Sabrina, can *you* skin a deer?"

I thought I had her, as there was no way she had skinned a deer before. The one thing she'd failed to do on the farm! But after a short, huffy pause, she zinged back at me,

> ANYONE CAN skin a deer. It just matters how long you take.

That statement pretty much changed my life.

It was so true. I could skin a deer. I don't like imagining it—the blood and guts and gore—but if the task in its simplest form was to take a knife and separate the skin from the rest of the body . . . I could do it. I had the physical capabilities of doing it. It might take way longer than a seasoned pro would take, and it might be way messier, but at the end of the day, I could get from point A to point B, from skinned to unskinned.

I didn't ask her, "Aunt Sabrina, can you skin a deer gracefully and efficiently and with minimal mess?" If I had, she would have had to say, "No, not on the first try."

This exchange made me realize that whenever I had a challenge or opportunity in front of me, I approached it by asking myself if I could do it, like, "Can I skin a deer?" And then, I realized, I would always silently tack on at the end, " . . . gracefully and efficiently and with minimal mess?" With that last question, no wonder it felt like I couldn't do much.

But if I took away that last part—"gracefully and efficiently and with minimal mess"—there was no end to what I could do! What things I could try! What challenges I could take on! Who cares if I made a mess?

Girls today get mixed messages. On the one hand, they're told they can do anything. On the other hand, there exists a pervasive message that whatever they do, it must be graceful and efficient and with minimal mess and minimal inconvenience to others. Girls (and women) get hardly any time or encouragement to make messes, learn on the go, and get by with the bare minimum if needed. You can do anything. Some of the things that you can do might be done awkwardly and ungracefully and messily at first, but you can still *do them*.

To move women forward in the world, we must accept that sometimes we'll do things ungracefully, and sometimes our sisters will do things ungracefully too, and that's okay! Let's get it done! Most times, it won't even matter if you did it awkwardly or gracefully, but that you *did it*. And if grace does matter, then the more you practice it, the more graceful you'll get anyway.

So next time you're wondering if you can do something, make sure you're not adding the silent conditions "gracefully and efficiently and with minimal mess," because that's nothing but the patriarchy holding you back.

9. Fear and Want

# CHAPTER 9
# Fear and Want

When I'm not sure what my next step is, instead of my old MO of freaking out, I like to do a journal exercise I call "Fear and Want." I came up with this handy trick when one day my mentor gave me a list of over 100 writing exercises and told me, "Don't worry, you don't need to do them all—just do the ones that truly appeal to you." Okay, great. "And," she continued, "do the ones you're really resisting." Hmmm . . .

I think about that moment often, because it holds so much wisdom. Going after what we love leads us to great things, and oftentimes, facing our fears also leads us to great things.

Taking this concept, I started to apply it to my whole life. Sometimes, I'll feel lost or restless—perhaps because I have nothing to do or perhaps because I have way too much to do. At times like these, I will whip out my journal and draw two big circles of a Venn diagram. One circle is "Fear" and the other circle is "Want." I'll write down everything I want and everything I fear, and if there's anything on both lists, I'll put it in the middle of the Venn diagram where Fear and Want overlap. That overlap is where the magic is.

Whatever I write in that overlap of Fear and Want is where I ought to concentrate my energies, because it's where I get the most bang for my buck. If you want it AND resist it at the same time, it means there's something special there. If you go after the thing you both fear *and* want, you will receive the greatest rewards.

Additionally, this exercise is great at reminding me: you can do anything, but you don't have to do everything. Whether or not you fear skydiving, if you don't want to do it, don't waste your time and money on it! You don't have to prove anything to anyone.

However, if you *do* want to go skydiving, and you also fear it, I'd advise you to head straight for the nearest skydiving facility. Anything that you both want and fear is something that takes up more space in your head than anything else. It means your Fearful Self has flagged it as something your subconscious cares deeply about, and responded to it by finding all the ways it could go wrong. Don't let that fabricated fear keep you from doing what you want. Let it guide you toward the things that will make you happiest.

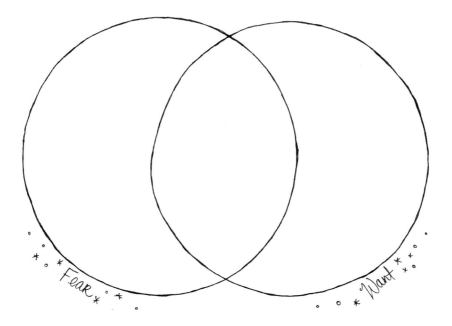

10. The Importance Scale

# CHAPTER 10
# The Importance Scale

At the International Bureau of Weights and Measures, they have a kilogram that is THE kilogram everything else is measured against. But in life, there is no such official scale of importance that we can consult to determine why what you find important is more important than what I find important, and vice versa. It is an impossible comparison.

Suppose you and I are going to have a discussion about "the important issues." Because there is no objective scale in existence, there is no official list of "important issues." For us to have a discussion, we'll have to share what we each find important rather than make assumptions about what the other finds important. We'll find the overlaps between what we each find important and have our discussion. If there is little to no overlap, and if I care about you or care about reaching an agreement with you, then I will decide that the issues you find important are important to me too, and you will do the same for me and my important issues.

The thing is, it's all too easy to fall under the spell of believing that there's an objective, overarching, official importance scale we all agree on. It's an illusion created by the patriarchy. But it's very enduring. When women and people of color have issues they deem important, those concerns are always somehow suspiciously deemed low by the patriarchy on the illusive objective importance scale. For example, we want reproductive rights, we want transgender rights, we don't want racial slurs. And if time and time again our issues rate "low" on the importance scale, we either 1) start accepting we are less important or 2) start getting suspicious of this so-called importance scale.

I used to be in camp 1. Now I am in camp 2.

If you buy into the existence of an objective importance scale, and your issues are always ranked low, then you might start using harmful tricks (harmful to YOU) in order to get your issue to rise on the scale. The patriarchy's scale says that tragedy is more important than joy. For example, I've heard of parents taking their kids out of school so they could attend a rock concert the parent found important and thought their kid would enjoy. But most of the time, the parents will say the child fell ill (tragedy) rather than that they were attending a concert (joy). The tragedy is excused more easily because tragedy is deemed to hold more weight than joy. So, knowing that tragedy is considered more "important" perhaps you make your situation sound bleaker than it is in order to focus attention on the issue you find important. No wonder the patriarchy complains about "hysterical women"—they created them, because they didn't find the non-hysterical woman's issue important, and she was forced to try to make her issue more important in their eyes via tragedy.

Here's another way the patriarchal importance scale skews the way we view things: I once read an article[2] about wealthy Canadian women who bought high-end fashion made by Canadian designers. At first blush, it might be easy to label these women as airy socialites who don't do much and just spend time buying expensive clothes that most people cannot afford. But this article pointed out that if it weren't for these women, these patrons, there would be no Canadian fashion design. When wealthy men buy art, they are art patrons. They are investing in art,

2 Maddeaux, S. (2014, November 14). "Here's to the ladies who lunch: How socialites are saving Canada's fashion industry, one soiree at a time." Retrieved from National Post: http://nationalpost.com/heres-to-the-ladies-who-lunch.

they are admired. When wealthy women buy fashion, they are superficial, self-centered airheads.

This is a case of the false importance scale that patriarchy has brainwashed us into thinking is an objective, unassailable FACT. We are so under its spell that many of us automatically judge the woman and praise the man because the woman is spending on something low on the false importance scale, while the man is spending on something high on the false importance scale—when really, remember, *there is no importance scale.*

It's gotten so bad that even simple pleasures—what we *like*—get skewed according to the importance scale. What women like is put low on the scale while what men like is put high on the scale. For example, any feminine interest is deemed a "guilty pleasure" (makeup, sweets, women-focused TV shows, etc.). *Monday Night Football* is not a guilty pleasure, just a pleasure that men have the right to enjoy. A guilty pleasure is when we like something that we're told isn't worthy of our attention or time or money or admiration because it's not very important—at least according to the false importance scale. And remember, *there is no importance scale.*

Have you ever read a business book or a conflict resolution book? I have. They're full of case studies like: "Bob and Bill are arguing about expanding the company to South America. They get nowhere until Bob admits that he is affraid of losing control of the company because the team will be scattered and he likes to be able to walk through the bullpen and talk to people and generate ideas. This is important to Bob. Once Bill understood what was important, they were able to agree, and they decide to expand to South America while keeping the core team at home."

Every case study is about a problem that starts because a group of people is operating on the false objective importance scale, and a resolution is only reached when that same group casts aside the patriarchy's false scale and gets honest, talking frankly about what is *really* essential and important to each of them.

So next time you feel hushed or silenced or ashamed about caring about something, whatever it is (*The Millionaire Matchmaker*, Planned Parenthood, Lush bath bombs), remember that there is no importance scale. If you find it important, it *is* important.

It's great to know what you find important and revel in that, but remember not to impose your importance scale on others. This is what people mean when they say "check your privilege." I always had trouble understanding the phrase until I realized that checking your privilege is simply making sure you note when your personal importance scale aligns with the patriarchy's importance scale, and that you don't confuse the two, i.e., you don't take your subjective importance scale and assume it is the objective importance scale, and—worse—then inflict it on others. Just as we want to try not to be a victim of the patriarchy's importance scale, we must strive to not be an abuser of it.

For example, let's say you work an office job and on your personal importance scale, working a nine-to-five office job is more steady, more responsible, more *important* than the work of an artist. You have an artist friend and you are trying to figure out a time and place to meet to catch up. You assume it is only natural for your friend to work around your schedule and meet you at a restaurant near your work for lunch. Your artist friend says that meeting up in the middle of the day interrupts her flow of creative work—can you meet for dinner or drinks instead? It is perfectly fine for you to say that meeting for dinner is inconvenient for you because you're tired after work and just want to go home. But if you were to say, "How dare you suggest we go out for cocktails at night—you know I work and have to get up early the next day! That is so irresponsible. Meeting up for lunch is the only sane way to catch up," then you are invoking your values of being a steady salaried worker (the patriarchy prioritizes steadiness and consistency—predictability, in other words) over that of your artist friend's more flexible work schedule. In other words, are you invoking your privilege of being aligned with the false patriarchy importance scale?

If you were to communicate honestly without invoking the patriarchy, perhaps your artist friend would agree to come to lunch with you because it's worth losing one day's work in order to catch up. And in this case, rather than sneering that this is how it should be since it is the "responsible" way, you will be grateful to her for compromising on her importance scale in order to accommodate your importance scale. Maybe lunch is on you. Even if you don't pay for lunch, the friendship is saved.

11. Hunting vs. Fishing

# CHAPTER 11
# Hunting vs. Fishing

*Disclaimer: I've never hunted. But when I think of* hunting, I think of how Ahab in *Moby-Dick* was obsessed with that one white whale and focused all of his attentions on that single prize. No other whale mattered.

Ahab was hunting, not fishing. Fishing is different. You sit in a boat or at the water's edge and you dip a bunch of lines in and wait for one to catch. Fishing makes me think of Huck Finn with a line tied around his big toe as he leans back and looks at the sky.

I think we attack life like it's a hunting game, when it's really more of a fishing game.

When you fish, you let loose a lot of bait (ideas) into the water, and you relax and chill and drink beer on the boat, and when one of the lines catches, you ride that baby out, hanging on to that fishing rod with all your might as you reel in your catch. And if none of your lines catch, you consider maybe it's the environment, so you move to a different area of the water and try your bait there. Or you try again another day. "The fish ain't biting today" is a saying for a reason.

In my field of screenwriting, everyone wants an agent, but there's no real 1-2-3-step way to do it. I've heard one screenwriter say that telling someone how to get an agent is like telling someone how to lose their virginity. There's no real way to do it. You can say, "Well, go to the dumpster behind the Walgreens . . . but that's probably not the best strategy."

What I tell writers who want an agent is that it's more like fishing, not hunting. Just like getting any job, you *can* hunt down an agent. In some ways, it's more exciting. You can look up the list of top agents in your genre and stalk this prey you've identified. You can scour Twitter until you've worked out their likes and dislikes, their common hangout spots, whether or not they have kids . . . Obviously, full-on stalker mode is discouraged, but if you're intent on knowing everything there is to know, you can do it. And the high achiever in you *likes* this way of doing things because it allows for fun schemes, and high drama, and most of all, it *feels like you're doing something.*

Fishing might feel like tearing your hair out for a high achiever like you. You just *wait.* Sure, you can get up early and get some good tackle, but after some activity bustling around, you wait. You get quiet. And that's torture. You can read a good book or play on your phone, but somehow this kind of activity feels less noble to you, High Achiever. A hunter in the woods silently tracking his prey is so much more epic than a fisherman playing on his phone on a nice day at the beach. Or is it? Waiting can be a big part of the epic, and it can reap epic results.

When it comes to many things, like getting an agent or getting a job, or finding a marriage partner, it's actually fishing that works better. You put out scripts (or résumés), you show up at networking events, and eventually, someone bites and you reel them in. If you're not getting many bites, you switch up the bait (scripts/résumés), and you switch up the watering holes. You get tips from other fishermen. You refine your idea of what you're looking for. And eventually you get an agent/job, and hopefully you find your partner in love.

So the thing is, now you have to answer the question really, really honestly: Is it more valuable to you to get an agent (or a marriage partner, or whatever success) . . . which requires you to fish and relax . . . or is it more valuable to you to feel important and be actively doing something, i.e., hunt?

Would you rather be seen as a noble hunter and never get anything to eat, or be seen as a slacker fisherman and eat well?

I want to add that it can be embarrassing to be a fisherman sometimes. People might call you a slacker or a failure. "Why don't you just give up?" "Why aren't you doing any work?"

But it's also really frustrating to be a hunter when it's not a hunting game.

I often think there's a breaking point when the frustration is so high that you decide to give embarrassment a try. And that's when the magic happens! That's when you start getting bites!

All the better if you figure it out early and skip the frustration part (hunting) and go right to the embarrassment part (fishing), knowing that this is a really advanced technique for getting what you want. Trust me.

12. Glide: The Work of Allowing

# CHAPTER 12
# Glide: The Work of Allowing

*I'm afraid of laziness. That sounds strange to admit,* but a lot of this book is about owning up to the tiny little fears that you put up with because someone told you they were useful, or inevitable, or things and situations you have to suck up and deal with. Laziness is one of those things, for me. It's why I spent so much of my formative years bearing down on project after project, putting in the hours, never letting an opportunity pass me by. And a lot of people will tell you that this work-all-the-time strategy is the correct way to go about your life, that constant work is the only way to get anywhere. The patriarchy will definitely encourage this theory. But that wasn't why I did it. I was afraid that if I ever stopped, or took a lengthy break, I'd never start again. I was afraid that my own laziness would prevent me from getting anything done, ever again.

You can see how ridiculous that is, right?

When I was a kid, my grandma would bring me to a pool for swimming lessons. It wasn't a big pool like you'd find at a community center or public pool—it was just the pool in a woman's backyard. The teacher was in her early thirties, and occasionally her mother would help out by occupying the group while her daughter worked through the one-on-ones. It was fairly basic stuff—you don't get a whole lot of motor control with six-year-olds—but they taught me how to float and get across the pool, teaching a very basic stroke they called Monkey, Starfish, Soldier.

I would float on my back and bend my limbs at the elbows and knees—Monkey. Then I would stretch my limbs spread eagle as far out as they could go—Starfish. And then (the most thrilling part for me), I would whoosh my arms to the sides and my legs would snap together to create a thrust of movement and my body would rocket forward—Soldier.

I would do this stroke over and over again as fast as I could. Monkey, Starfish, Soldier, Monkey, Starfish, Soldier, Monkey—and inevitably I would get screamed at. Both by the teacher and the teacher's mother: "GLIDE! Krista, you have to GLIDE! You're doing it wrong, GLIDE!"

I didn't understand. The quicker I went through the motions without stopping, the faster I would go, right? What was with their obsession with "gliding"? That would only slow me down!

I ignored them lesson after lesson. They grew really worried about me and started giving me lots of one-on-one pep talks, explaining the importance of gliding. "You're doing all this work, Krista, but you don't let it carry you as far as it can. Instead, you stop the glide from Solider and hop right back into Monkey again. If you keep doing this you'll get tired sooner and not get as far. If you allow yourself to glide, you'll go farther faster."

Hmmmm . . . I mean . . . going farther faster sounded really good to me, but this whole gliding business? It went against everything I was taught! But one day they wore me down, and I tried it. I went from Monkey to Starfish to Soldier, and after I did Soldier, I let the thrust of my motions carry my body through the water. I quelled the itch to go right back into Monkey and just let my body be, feeling it move like a missile, going farther than I realized my Soldier stroke could take me, and then . . . I felt it. A pause. A slight slowdown. And then I knew, *that* was the time to go into Monkey and begin the process anew. My swim teacher and her mother cheered and wept (well, they didn't weep, but I'd like to think they felt really satisfied by a teaching job well done).

Just as in the swimming pool, so it is in life. You might be running around like crazy, afraid that if you were to stop for just a moment, your life would come to a standstill and you would never break through the inertia to start again. And you would wither and die, rooted in that spot. So . . . you keep on going, scurrying on that hamster wheel, running that rat race, furiously going from Monkey to Starfish to Soldier and back again . . . but if you give the glide a chance, you'll see that when you pause your frenzied strokes and allow yourself to glide, you'll go far, fast, with no effort . . . and you'll also find that your body will *feel* when it is time to move again, and your muscles will be *eager* to do so. You are in no danger of the dreaded laziness, because you're enjoying yourself in these movements.

When you're on an extended vacation, you might find that after some rest and relaxation, good ole R&R, you start feeling . . . antsy. You don't want to lie down in a hammock by the ocean, you want to *move* and *talk* and *create*. That's your body at the end of a glide, telling you it's time to make waves again.

Your body will tell you many inconvenient things, most of which we usually overlook completely. One of these things is that work and rest are part of the same cycle, just like thrusting your arm through water and gliding are part of the same stroke. Trying to swim without allowing yourself to glide will get you the same results I got when I was a kid: yards behind my classmates, and twice as tired. Your body will tell you when you need to glide, just like it knows when you need to focus.

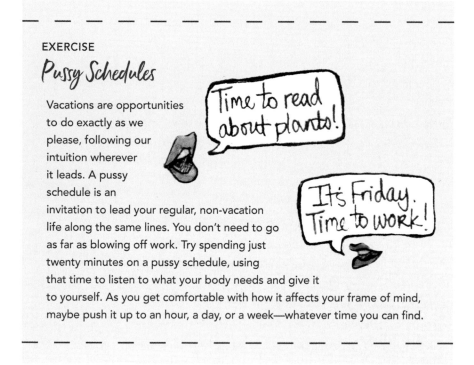

**EXERCISE**

## *Pussy Schedules*

Vacations are opportunities to do exactly as we please, following our intuition wherever it leads. A pussy schedule is an invitation to lead your regular, non-vacation life along the same lines. You don't need to go as far as blowing off work. Try spending just twenty minutes on a pussy schedule, using that time to listen to what your body needs and give it to yourself. As you get comfortable with how it affects your frame of mind, maybe push it up to an hour, a day, or a week—whatever time you can find.

The scary part is being confident enough in listening to your body to communicate its needs to other people. How are you supposed to deal with deadlines or meetings or other people's needs if you wake up one morning and hear your body whisper "glide" at you? As with everything, discernment is key. If your schedule is flexible—if you're working freelance or you own your own business, say—there's no real reason why you can't mold your life to fit whichever mode you're in, even if, to an outside observer, it *looks* lazy. You know your own needs best, and you know that no matter how relaxed you get, your dreams and ambitions will inevitably pull you back to work.

If it's less flexible—if you have to be at work every day at 8:30 a.m.—try to mold that schedule to fit your gliding self. If you're often tired in the mornings (for instance), don't schedule a bunch of hard things for that time slot. Expect a little less of yourself at that hour, and try to figure out the best way to communicate the way you and your body work to other people. Historically, employer demands on your time have been rooted in an industrial age emphasis on mechanical consistency, but you are not a machine. It's okay to trust and nourish your body-mind, provided you can effectively communicate your needs to your coworkers.

13. Self-care vs. Self-help

# CHAPTER 13
# Self-care vs. Self-help

There is a crucial difference between self-care and self-help. Self-help is important. It's when you are down and out and need to build yourself back up, often through pleasure and pampering and joy (let's call it PPJ for now). A lot of women are told that we need to be better about this. And we are getting better at it. The next step, though, is giving ourselves PPJ even when we are *not* down and out. Even if we're just fine. Because if you only give yourself PPJ when you're down and out, what are you teaching yourself? That you only get PPJ when you're down and out! So we need to be administering PPJ even when we're also *up*. Because that is the only way we will *rise*.

When you give yourself PPJ, when you schedule it into your routine, even when you don't "need" it, that is not just self-help, that is *true* self-care!

Self-care is so important, I think of it like maintaining brake pads on a car. When I lived in New York City, sometimes as I entered the subway I would hear the train and narrowly miss it. On some days, I would just shrug, take a step back, and wait patiently for the next train. On other days,

I would be on the verge of tears, and the ten-minute wait for the next train would feel insufferable. It made me wonder, why is it on some days missing the train feels like nothing, yet on other days it feels like the last straw to a breakdown? The answer is brake pads. When I was doing good self-care, I had thick brake pads. Missing the train was like hitting the brake pads to my good day, but because the pads were thick, it was a smooth, silent, safe stop. But when I wasn't doing self-care and had thin brake pads, missing the train was like hitting the brakes and hearing that piercing squeal—super-stressful.

So make sure you do your self-care, even when you're not in crisis. Maintaining thick brake pads allows you to handle moments in life when you have to "hit the brakes" with grace and cheeriness. With self-care, you'll be out and about changing the world with a smile on your face.

# CHAPTER 14
# Idea Squelchers vs. Idea Nurturers

*I was raised with a very specific idea of what a correct* path in life is: I was to be either a physician, or a lawyer, or a professor, or maybe all three. When I told my parents that I wanted to be a writer, an uncertain pause followed. I still remember the exchange of glances as my parents tried to figure out how to make their daughter snap out of this obviously dangerous fantasy. The dangers included, but were not limited to: social humiliation, empty bank accounts, relationships with boys of similar penniless writer ilk, divorce, more social humiliation, family shame, dying without any children or accomplishment to be proud of. Couldn't their daughter see that all of these dangers could be avoided simply by becoming a physician, a lawyer, a professor, or all three?

But I didn't want to be a physician. Or a lawyer. Or a professor. So I live with that uncertain fearful pause, full of dangers and shame, and every time I put pen to paper, I have to shoo away the squelchers it spawns. *You don't know what you're talking about. Someone smarter already did a better version of this. This job is just make-believe, isn't it?* But shooing them away is not enough. I have to actively nurture my ideas.

Here's the thing about ideas. They start out like babies: cute, clueless, and totally incapable of fending for themselves. Have you ever see the scrap paper of an inventor? Full of ridiculous doodles that should never see the light of day. Prototypes are usually riddled with mistakes and miscalculations. For example, early beta versions of video games are often stuffed with awkward bugs and weird, inside jokes the designer threw in at 2:00 a.m. because it *seemed* like a reasonable thing to do. As a whole, ideas start out goofy and meandering, and even if they start out full of energy, they tend to be incomplete. They need time and attention to develop into a mind-bending story or an economy-disrupting invention or a genre-busting game. Or a world-changing event.

Now, nurturing an idea takes time and energy, so whatever proto-idea you choose, make sure that you *love* it. Even if the squelchers tell you the idea is dumb-as-toast. If you choose an idea that you're only sort of lukewarm about, but the squelchers are quiet on, you're just letting yourself be held hostage by your self-doubt. Listen to yourself, and when you get an idea that you keep circling back to because there's something about it that scratches you in juuuust the right place, you've found the idea you're going to develop. At that point, your work begins.

The idea for the Pussyhat Project had humble beginnings. When I first made plans in November to attend the Women's March, I was focused on just what *I* could do, what sign *I* could hold, what clothes *I* could wear that could visually express what I was feeling and how I wanted the world to change. I figured just one iconic photo could make a huge impact in this visual, Internet-savvy world we live in, but I couldn't think of anything. Until I realized that as an L.A. girl, I'd be really cold in DC during the winter. A coat wasn't a decorative accessory; it was a must. I'd have to button it up all the way and seal the cracks with gloves, a scarf, and a hat. Because knitting was my latest obsession, it occurred to me that I could knit a hat for myself, and that making the hat for the march with my own two hands was meaningful. This is where things got exciting. The idea came to me all at once. As much as I love knitting, I'm still very much a beginner knitter, and I thought, *If I can knit this hat, anyone can.* And if I shared the pattern, we could all make these hats and either wear them ourselves or send them to someone attending the march. Because the hats were on top of people's heads, from an aerial view, the gathered crowd would create an ocean of pink. Even on that day in November, imagining it, I felt the impact. I'd started by wanting a symbol to express myself, and it turned into a huge community art project.

This was the moment. The moment I could have given up and given in to the squelchers. This idea was particularly ripe for squelching: by the patriarchy, by my family, by my own inner voice. I am so glad I didn't give in to the squelchers. When you have your moment and need to decide, "Do I squelch or do I nurture?" I hope you put on your pussyhat and choose "nurture."

15. Find Yourself Fascinating:
A Personal Inventory

CHAPTER 15

# Find Yourself Fascinating: A Personal Inventory

CARING FOR MYSELF IS NOT SELF-INDULGENCE,
IT IS SELF-PRESERVATION, AND THAT IS AN
ACT OF POLITICAL WARFARE.

—Audre Lorde

I used to keep myself really blank. I would not commit to any preferences or hold any opinions. In truth, I was afraid of making any choices. I was fearful even of choosing a favorite color. Why so afraid? Because I didn't want to shut down any potential options or be stuck with just one thing.

As I grew older, though, I wondered if maybe I was afraid of choosing a favorite because I wanted to be perennially likable. What if I chose blue, and the person who asked the question didn't like blue? Safer to just say, "I don't know, I don't have a favorite." I always wanted to have the right answer, the one that would make the other person like me.

As a student, I was really good at sussing out what my teachers wanted, what would get me an "A." When I started going out on dates, I admired my own chameleon qualities. I was really good at determining what my date wanted in a woman, and I could become her, mostly because I was blank to begin with. It was a thrilling game, one I relished getting good at.

That's why I call this state "blank check." "Blank" sounds horrifying—a cavernous empty void—but "blank check" sounds so powerful, full of possibility. If you have the idea that you are blank then you can be *any-thing*, and that potential can feel thrilling. You can be anything for any-one, and that's what is dangerous about this state; it's enticing. Women are rewarded for accommodating others, especially men, and the best blank check-ers get rewarded the most. Oftentimes the reward is a "good" reputa-tion, or sometimes just the absence of monikers like "bitch," "demanding," and "crazy."

But it's not so fun when you do something like apply for college, or write an autobiography for an application to a grant or job or prize you really want, where it helps to stand out, know yourself, and be fascinating. That's hard when you can't even pick a favorite color, much less know what you stand for in this world and what drives you, what delights you, what fasci-nates you. It also can make it hard to just be by yourself. Being a blank check creates an unease in your own body because you don't really know yourself.

It can be scary to have an opinion, especially as a woman. Because once you have an opinion, you no longer have the safety of the blank check. Once you have an opinion, you can be argued with, disliked, hated even. But it's so frustrating—even heartbreaking—to feel like you're blending in with everyone else when deep down you *know* you are unique, interesting, fascinating, and somehow it's not coming through. It's because you are being the blank check.

You'll often see trends of what opinions are "safe" to have, such as, "If you wear a short skirt you ought to balance it out with a long-sleeved top" and "Wine, coffee, and dogs make my day go round," "I really want to travel one day," "I love naps." If you adopt these, you aren't standing out, so you're still a blank check. But who wants to be a person whose likes and dislikes are defined by the latest conventional wisdom hitting the newsfeed?

Pick favorites. Know you can change your mind. I dare you—fill in your blank check with a preference, and start living.

KNOW YOURSELF.

In the process of knowing thyself, you gotta start somewhere, and even knowing your favorite flavor of coffee is a start.

I can't express enough how liberating it is to start having opinions over the most mundane things. What is my favorite Starbucks? (London Fog Latte.) What is my favorite bubble bath? (Lush French Kiss.) What is my favorite movie? (*Strictly Ballroom.*)

What do you *like*? Knowing what you like is a kind of superpower. Who knew, right? It's why the patriarchy has discouraged it for so long.

Feminists from earlier generations encouraged using a mirror to examine your vulva/vagina/crotch/pussy in order to really SEE it. This "mirror exercise" grew out of the fact that many women at that time didn't feel comfortable looking at their bodies, and they definitely had NOT been encouraged to explore/appreciate/know their vaginas.

The possibility of sexual pleasure aside (so many other brilliant writers have explored its relevance to personal freedom and self-knowledge), knowing what you like—in terms of food preferences, maybe, or taste in poetry—is incredibly powerful. A woman who knows what she likes (and, by extension, what she doesn't like) is hideous to the patriarchy, because knowing that is the first step to having agency. Sally ordering a meal—in precisely the way she liked it—in the film *When Harry Met Sally* was often met with disbelief and derision. Why can't she just order like everyone else? Why start a fuss?

That's where it begins. It's in those small, seemingly insignificant moments (like ordering a burger) when we're asked to put aside our desires that we begin to lose our agency for life's bigger decisions. "Why can't you just go along with what everyone else is doing/saying/thinking?" And that's when the patriarchy takes over guiding women's decisions, setting the course of their lives, determining how they feel/think/act/look/ move. On the other hand, a woman who knows what she wants? Yeah, she's not going to let anyone else determine how she lives her life.

In short, self-knowledge is so powerful that people who possess power discourage those who have less power to try to own it, understand it, or claim it. One of the ways in which we lose our power is simple: we're made to feel guilty for finding ourselves fascinating.

When women look inside themselves (literally with a mirror, or metaphorically!), we might initially be branded as "self-centered," "self-obsessed," "superficial," or "selfish." Sound familiar? It likely does. I say: study yourself anyway. Get to know yourself and get comfortable with yourself. Because if you're going to change the world, in addition to fulfilling your own dreams, it helps immeasurably if you know yourself, what you're good at, and how you work best. That way, when you DO work with other people, you are the best possible collaborator. The best teams, like so many I've been lucky enough to be a part of, are composed of people who know themselves; the ones who have done the "selfish" work of turning inward and sorting things out for themselves. The worst people to work with are the ones who are unaware of who they are and what makes them tick; those who have NOT done the (so-called) "selfish," "self-obsessed" work of getting to know themselves. Ironically, these selfless folk often become the most egotistical burden on the team.

I love the quote I used at the beginning of this chapter from poet and activist and badass woman Audre Lorde about the transformative power of self-care. I would add to it that DOCUMENTING YOURSELF is not self-indulgence, it is self-preservation, and *that* is an act of political warfare. Finding yourself fascinating is important.

It matters because:

1. It's fun and enjoyable, which is, well . . . FUN. Why else are you here in the world? When you don't have your iPhone and you don't have your TV and you don't have people-watching to occupy your time, all you have is yourself. When you find yourself fascinating, as you no doubt are, that's all you need to be entertained and lively. There's an old saying—be your own best friend—and it applies here.

2. When you know yourself, you're better able to collaborate with others and make great change . . . and why else are you here in the world if not to make a unique contribution?

Here are some ways to document yourself and do a practice I like to call "taking your own inventory":

Take quizzes! I like these:
- Myers-Briggs
- StrengthsFinder 2.0
- Five Love Languages
- How to Fascinate
- Enneagram

Make lists!
- Books I've read this year
- New restaurants I've visited this year

# 12 Houses

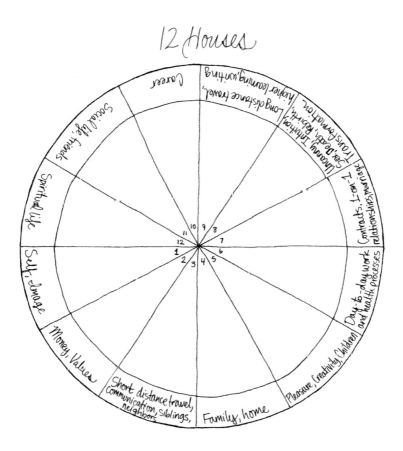

Journal! Here are some prompts I use frequently when journaling:

- **Your Body:** Draw your body (can be a stick figure) and then write down all the information you know about yourself when it comes to each body part.

- **12 Houses Check-up:** I also use the categories of astrology as an overall way to check in on my life, see what's going well, and to find places where things might be going better. Using each house as a prompt, write out an assessment of how things in your life are going according to these categories.

*House 1:* Self, image
*House 2:* Money, values
*House 3:* Short-distance travel, communication, siblings, neighbors
*House 4:* Family, home
*House 5:* Pleasure, creativity, children
*House 6:* Day-to-day work and health processes
*House 7:* Contracts, one-on-one relationships, marriage
*House 8:* The uncanny, intuition, sex, death, rebirth, transformation
*House 9:* Long-distance travel, higher learning, writing
*House 10:* Career
*House 11:* Social life, friends
*House 12:* Spiritual life

♥ **Write a Love Letter to Yourself:** Write a gushing romantic note like one you would want a lover to write to you. Be sexy, be bold, be adoring, be coy. Flirt with yourself, compliment yourself, try to win yourself over, body and mind, with the written word.

As you make note of all these fascinating facts about you and the opinions you have, it's important not to judge yourself on your responses or create a "grass is always greener on the other side" situation. For example, if you have curly hair, celebrate it, and don't feel bad that you don't have straight hair. For straight-haired gals, don't envy the girls with curly hair. There's no one right way to be. Whatever you are at the moment, embrace it!

EXERCISE

## Chick-Lit Heroine Exercise

This journaling exercise helps you see yourself as the hero of your own fascinating story. The first paragraph is all about the details of your life. Too often, we stop seeing the life we have as fascinating. By writing yourself as a character, you start to see that you ARE fascinating—the way you live, the objects you own, the town you live in—it's all fresh and new to *somebody* out there. You might think that your hometown is boring, but it'll be fascinating to others. I love reading chick lit set in New York City, Omaha, Shanghai, pretty much anywhere in the world!

When asked for an adjective describing you at your best and an adjective describing you at your worst, you are presenting you as a *whole* person, and a person with highs and lows is a fascinating character. If you didn't have flaws you wouldn't be fascinating. (In fact, you wouldn't be human, so you might simply be an interesting robot, which is not nearly as interesting.)

The second paragraph is all about what you want and what you need, and what's stopping you from getting that. Sometimes what's stopping you is external (mean boss, distant boyfriend, no money), and sometimes it's internal (no self-confidence, fear of failure). So often it's the case that what we want and what we need are vastly different. The excitement in your story comes from exploring your wants and your needs. In the second paragraph, we learn to see our problems as adventures, and we all know chick lit has a happy ending, so we learn to avoid despair because we know somehow, our problem-adventures will have a happy ending. As John Lennon said, "Everything will be okay in the end. If it's not okay, it's not the end."

Give it a shot!

_____ _____ is a _____ yet
<your first name>    <your last name>    <adjective describing you at your best>

_____    _____
<adjective describing you at your worst>    <your occupation (e.g. doctor, teacher, homemaker, student)>

living in her _____ in the
                    <your type of residence (e.g. mansion, apartment, house, estate, dorm)>

_____    _____
<adjective describing your town>    <noun describing your climate or community (e.g. fields, delta,
                                        downtown, forest, neighborhood)>

of _____, _____ (home of the _____ ) along
    <your city>    <your state>                <thing/event/food item your town is known for>

with her _____    _____
                <adjective describing person you live with, if any>    <occupation of the person you live with, if any>

_____ her
<relationship of the person you live with to you, if any (husband, roommate, etc.)>

collection of _____ , and her prized
                    <thing you collect or own a lot of>

_____ .
    <your best species and pet name or most prized object (e.g. dog Suzy, parrot Andrew, Mustang convertible)>

She wants _____ , in order to
                <thing, accomplishment, or relationship you really want right now>

_____ , but what holds her back is
<why do you really want that right now, what will it lead to>

_____ . As she valiantly continues
<what is holding you back from having/taking the thing you want>

her journey along with her _____ -obsessed
                                    <activity/hobby/thing your best friend is obsessed with>

best friend and despite her enemy _____ ,
                                            <name of your enemy (e.g. Patricia, the patriarchy,
                                                the housing board)>

she might just find that what she really needs is _____ .
                                                        <what you suspect you really need to learn>

When I start to feel boring, inert, inactive, it makes me less likely to take bold action and speak up for the change I want to see in the world. When that happens, the patriarchy scores a win. I use the fill-in-the-blank exercise to remind myself that I am a fascinating person with a fascinating story, and that no matter what, I have a unique contribution to make to the world. This exercise also reframes problems as challenges and story arcs, which provides distance from the emotions associated with them. When you can examine a situation from a distance, you can usually make more sense of it, because you've got a bird's-eye view, an objective look.

For instance, when it comes to your work style, maybe you are a sprinter or maybe you are a marathoner. I am more of a sprinter—I'm at my best when I'm writing quickly and in concentrated bursts. I love a good high-pressure situation, and I love making decisions quickly. Sometimes I bemoan not being more of a respectable marathoner, but I found that this attitude can make you crazy—when you become a marathoner you suddenly wish you were a sprinter, when you're a sprinter you wish you were a marathoner, and on and on and on. You can save yourself from the stress of always wanting to be something that you aren't by pointing out to yourself from the get-go: curly is valid, straight is valid, sprinting is valid, marathoning is valid. All ways are valid. When you make a personal inventory, don't judge yourself, simply take inventory. This is about knowledge, not judgment.

My next recommended step for you is to share your inventory about your fascinating self with someone else. This can be fun, and honestly, it can also be very helpful to someone out there to know and see that they are less alone, and to encourage them to write their own inventories.

For instance, in the Broadway musical *Fun Home*, the most touching song for me was "Ring of Keys." In this scene, Young Alison sees a delivery woman dressed in a particular masculine way, a way she'd never seen before, and while the two characters don't directly interact, this delivery woman made a huge impression on Young Alison. Because she had short hair and wore dungarees, it was the first time Alison saw herself reflected in the world, and that fact alone was fundamental, as it made her feel less alone. And when we don't feel alone, we feel more capable, more motivated, more supported. What's amazing is that *you* could be that delivery woman. Just by being authentic, just by being yourself in the world, you too could inspire someone as you go about your day. Sharing your personal inventory works similarly. Every presentation—visually or verbally or otherwise—is a method of sharing that can unite and empower us.

When we see someone we know, we feel known as well, and seen.

16. Weapon to Warrior

# CHAPTER 16
# Weapon to Warrior

I was dating a television reporter and we were having breakfast one morning—madeleines and blueberry muffins at my local Coffee Bean & Tea Leaf. We were both twenty-nine. I've dated men who were twenty-two and men who were fifty-five, though generally on the older end of the spectrum, but never someone my age; in this case, EXACTLY my age.

He was returning to Paris that day, and I wasn't sure when I'd see him again. I could feel both of us drifting apart already. I suddenly *beheld* him, as if from a distance, and was amazed. He was a wonderful, successful person, but unlike some of the older guys I had dated, he was only just beginning; there was more he was going to do for the world . . .

"I can't wait to see what you become," I blurted out. He stared at me. I tried to explain without sounding like I was putting myself above him, judging his progress like some teacher I wasn't. "It's like, you're blossoming." He was silent. Too feminine maybe, I thought, so I tried again. "Or, you know, evolving."

He brightened. "You mean, like a Pokémon?"

Now it was my turn to be silent.

"Yes," I finally said. "Like a Pokémon."

We had a delightful conversation about what type of Pokémon he would be. (I said he'd be super cute; he said he'd have awesome badass skills.)

"Do you feel like a Pokémon at work?" I asked.

He stared at me, gobsmacked. "You know, that is the perfect way to describe it." He mimicked throwing a Pokéball. "Pokémon, *report*!"

We parted, and to this day, I'm itching to tell him more, all about my theory of the Weapon and the Warrior as it formed in my head.

This is the theory: We all have to make the leap (the evolution, the blossoming) from weapon to warrior. From object to subject.

If I were to ask you, "Do you want to be objectified?" you'd say *hell no*. You're way too smart for that.

But the weapon to warrior path is so tricky, because the thing about being a weapon is, it's *cool*. What if I were to ask you, "Do you want to be an amazing weapon? You would be so powerful, so dangerous . . . " It's enticing. There is glee and power in the idea of being the most awesome weapon you can imagine.

In high school and into my twenties, I loved packing my résumé with accolades and feeling awesome. Every time I was hired, I wanted to be the nuclear option of weapons. I wanted to say: hire me to write your screenplay, plan your party, fix your problem, I WILL GET IT DONE. I had dreams of being the most badass assistant in the world—I imagined I would be able to fly planes, ride motorcycles, speak many languages, and all the while I'd look beautiful and sexy and intimidating. Everyone would envy any employer who could afford me.

On a more mundane, less fantastical level, there is a thrill to being useful. As women, we're taught all our lives to be of use; we're told there is great value in striving to be a productive member of society. We're taught to be weapons; but at the end of the day, a weapon is a tool. And as is true with a weapon, it's important who wields it, and for what, and why.

Trying to be the best you can be is a noble pursuit, but if you are being the best you can be in order to be *used* by other people, then you are the weapon, not the warrior. Shifting into Warrior Mode is scary, because while you can be the perfect weapon, you can never be the perfect warrior. Warriors are human, and humans make mistakes. And we've been taught, especially as women, that mistakes are NOT GOOD. So no wonder we stick to being awesome weapons. No wonder we're more comfortable serving as the tools that enable other people to fight their most important battles.

Let me ask you these questions: Why do you work so hard? Why did you keep yourself in school for as long as you did? Why do you push yourself to gain new skills? Why are you always pushing yourself to be better, stronger, more successful, more (fill in the adjective of your choice). If you're like me, it's so you can be prepared for whatever might come your way—whether it's an interview for your dream job or a first date. I've always taken pride in doing something well, and I loved the idea of being someone's dream, of being exactly what they needed. If my boss needed me to write a report, I loved being able to hand in the best damn report he'd ever seen. If she wanted me to give a presentation on our latest project, I wanted to deliver something that would excite our allies and convince our opponents. Whatever it was, I wanted to be a perfect fit. I wanted to put my years of study and dedication into my job, and see all the work move mountains, make magic.

I wanted to be the perfect weapon.

There's a kind of peace in that idealized place. When someone else—your boss or a friend, maybe—needs you to do something, there's no need for self-doubt, fear of consequences, or anxiety over whether completing that task will bring you closer to your goals. It's someone else's play, which also means it's someone else's blowback, someone else's responsibility. The only thing that concerns you, really, is doing the thing as magnificently as possible. You get all the action and none of the blame. Being someone else's weapon can be profoundly liberating. It can also be limiting. Why?

Because while there's power in being someone's weapon, that power isn't dedicated to fulfilling your own desires. While, in the short term, women are often rewarded for concealing their opinions, goals, or dreams, in the long term, we suffer. Ceding responsibility for yourself to another person—being the weapon that is *yielded*—can erode your sense of identity, and even impede your ability to accurately value yourself.

That's why it's important to know when to shift from Weapon Mode into Warrior Mode. Warrior Mode is what I call that place of knowing exactly why you're doing something, a mode in which you're doing what you're doing specifically to further *your* goals and nobody else's. You're using all the skills and education and experience you've accumulated to benefit *yourself*, to pursue *your* dreams. Any mountain you move, you're moving because *you* need it out of the way. Warrior Mode is about taking control of and responsibility for your actions.

The process of shifting into Warrior Mode can be scary, in part because you might be entering unknown territory, an unknown way of acting or thinking or being or even seeing the world. No matter how much you sugarcoat it, the truth is that perfectionism is rooted in fear—the fear that a single mistake will cost us money or respect or opportunities. That fear is heightened when you're the one steering the course and in charge of the action. When you're fighting for yourself, the stakes are always higher, and the risks feel more precarious.

For me, the Pussyhat Project was the biggest endeavor I'd ever attempted, and it was terrifying. There were so many ways it could go wrong. There was so much potential for criticism. But I also knew that no one else was going to do it. I had all the skills necessary—I was armed with knitting needles and a certain amount of media savvy—and the only way it was going to happen was if I stepped out of being a perfect weapon and became the warrior that the project needed.

When you are the warrior, you must decide for yourself to what causes you will lend your skill. I received an unmarked package from a woman who sent in a pussyhat. She apologized for not including a return address, admitting that she was afraid her husband would find out she had knit a pussyhat. I imagine she is a weapon for her husband in many ways; perhaps she's knitted sweaters as Christmas presents to his relatives. She has this skill of knitting, and this time, she decided to deploy her skill for herself; she became a warrior and made a pussyhat because it represented a cause she believes in, a cause that not everyone around her supports.

So, are you the weapon or the warrior? You are fully capable of being either, any time you please.

Or, if you prefer, are you the Pokémon, or the Pokémon master?

17. I, Object

# CHAPTER 17
# I, Object

The patriarchy is tricky when it comes to objectifying women. We are people, not objects, but with all the messages we receive about our bodies and our options and what we should or shouldn't think or do, it can be difficult to remember that. Women are constantly being objectified, and not just in the way you think. Although women are getting better at pointing out the injustice of being turned into a sexual object, we are constantly allowing ourselves to be turned into a utility object.

It's kind of like tricking a kid on the playground.

"Oh well, I guess you don't really want to (something awesome), what was I thinking? That you actually WANT to help people? My mistake. I thought that you are actually smart and capable! Ha! Silly me. I never should have believed you were a good, strong, per—"

That's when the kid jumps up and takes the bait. "No, I AM smart and capable. No, I CAN do this. Watch! I'll show you!"

It's the oldest trick in the book, and I've fallen for it. Maybe you have too. The trick has to do with making objectification sound more fun than it is.

A blank check seems rife with possibilities (it's still an object). A weapon seems powerful (it's still an object).

We want to be useful, and that is noble, but we must remember we get to choose when and how we want to be useful. We never *have* to do anything. There is no "right" way, only the way that feels right to us.

I am not a blank check. I am not a weapon. I am not a gumball machine.

I think about that a lot lately. In the wake of the Pussyhat Project, I felt like I was a defective gumball machine. I felt the pressure of "Here! Stick a social injustice coin in her, and she'll spit out a colorful activism project candy!" People were asking for the candy, shoving the social injustice coins in my face, and I didn't blame them, they were totally right to ask. But I felt such a deep disappointment in myself until I realized . . . I am not a gumball machine, I am an artist, I am a *person*. It's okay if things take time to generate. It's okay if, rather than Pussyhat Project 2.0, I decide that I want to write a book teaching people ways to liberate their thinking and create their own activism projects. It's not the candy promised by the gumball machine, but it's what the artist in my heart yearns to create.

We are not utility objects, we are not utility machines. And that's okay. That's wonderful!

A note: It is fine to sometimes enjoy the thrill of being a well-oiled machine. It's a wide-eyed compliment we often give people. "You're a machine!" "Wow, you finished that so quickly?! You're a godsend!"

Enjoy it, but don't forget that the minute you want to stop, that is *your* choice. I think too often women enjoy being utility objects (which is *fine*) but then forget it is their choice to stop whenever they feel like it. Perhaps they fear they won't be loved anymore if they stop being the machine. Pay attention to when this might be happening to you.

- - - - - - - - - - - - - - - - - - - -

EXERCISE

## Owning Your Objectification

Write down three ways you are useful to others. (Thank you for serving others!)

1.

2.

3.

For each way you are useful, come up with an object as a metaphor for what you do. (For example, if you feed a whole army of kids, maybe you are a vending machine. If you lend money to relatives, maybe you are an ATM.)

1.

2.

3.

For each metaphorical object that you are being, write down a reason why you LOVE being this machine. (For example, I love being a vending machine because hungry people are so excited to see their favorite snack in me, and I know they need a pick-me-up, a break away from their tedious computer work.) Really rest in the glow of that, appreciate the service you offer. Don't judge it! Embrace it.

1.

2.

3.

This is a great exercise to point out how you ought to pat yourself on the back more often, without judgment or shame (e.g., rather than beating yourself up for being an object, celebrate how you have been making the world a better place!). An added bonus of the exercise is that you are made aware of your "weak points" and have transformed them into your strong points. What I mean by this is, in the future, when the patriarchy is trying to pull that ol' trick on you ("Oh, I guess you don't like to make people happy and I guess you don't like helping the hungry and I guess you don't make delicious things appear after all"), instead of being like, "No, wait! I DO want to make people happy and help the hungry and I DO make delicious things, let me show you, " you can say, "I *know* I do that, and I enjoy doing that, but I choose not to for your particular cause."

Lastly, for each metaphorical object you enjoy being, write down *who* you really are using these fill in the blanks: e.g., while I love that I can be a gumball machine and transform a problem into a colorful opportunity, at the end of the day, I am not a gumball machine, I am an artist.

> While I love that I can be a _vending machine_ and _provide people a_
> _delicious break_, at the end of the day, I am not a vending machine,
> I am a chef.

By the way, if you're not sure "who" you really are (artist, chef, etc.) a "who" that always works is "person:"

I am not a vending machine, I am a person.

I am not a gumball machine, I am a person.

1.

2.

3.

18. Athena Complex

# CHAPTER 18
# Athena Complex

*Athena is the goddess of wisdom in Greek mythology.* Zeus, her father, gave birth to her from his head, and she emerged fully formed. Yes, you read that right, she emerged a fully formed adult goddess—in other words, she was *perfect*. She gestated in his head, and banged out her own shield in the process, which gave her father a headache.

I used to try to be Athena in everything I did. When I decided to become a writer, I wanted to hide away (like in a cave, or in Zeus's head) and bang away at it, and not come out into the world until I was a fully formed, perfect, unimpeachable, totally expert, and award-winning writer. If I ever needed to learn a skill like tennis (which up to this point I've never had to, thankfully, because I'd be terrible at it), my ideal plan would be something like this: Go to a town where nobody knows me and hire an instructor who is sworn to secrecy and signs a nondisclosure agreement agreeing to NEVER talk about how clumsy I was when I started out. Then we'd close down the tennis court to all intruders and board up the windows, and then we would meet every day for three months, during which time I would live and breathe tennis. Then, when I was "perfect," I would come home and go on that first date with a guy who suggested we play tennis three months ago. And I would win every match.

Phew. I mean, that's so EXHAUSTING. Especially when I was trying to apply that to EVERYTHING I was doing in my life, from learning how to do makeup to learning how to write. The nature of creativity dictates that you must make mistakes. Using my self-imposed Athena Complex, escaping to "hermit mountain" was the way around that. I thought, well, if mistakes are inevitable . . . I'll just *do my mistakes in private* and it'll be like it never happened. I will find a way to be perfect, which will mean I'll never be embarrassed. I'll always be okay.

However, as embarrassing as it might feel while we're going through it, we learn so much by airing our mistakes in public. We learn so much about just trying things, and possibly failing, and then trying again. As Samuel Beckett used to say, "Ever tried. Ever failed. No matter. Try again. Fail again. Fail better." We gain so much when we share our work, even when it is on feeble fawn legs. Comedians, actors, and writers call it feedback. And although it can often feel like torture, it definitely helps us grow.

Also, if we adhere to the Athena Complex too much, we may never release anything, never grow, never give our creations a chance to become accomplishments and beloved pieces of art for others to enjoy. In other words, if we're going to make our unique mark in the world, we're going to make mistakes. Lots of them.

We can let go of the Athena Complex and eschew perfectionism, which may be more difficult than it sounds.

Why? Because we're likely all guilty of perfectionism, I'm sure. Have you ever held back on showing someone your work because you thought it wasn't perfect? You might worry about sharing your creation because you feel the creation represents you, and you don't want the person or critic to see you as less than perfect.

The heart of perfectionism, that running tape in your head speaking to you, is this: I'm afraid if I am less than perfect, people will criticize me (or embarrass me, or not hire me, or reject me, or speak badly of me to others . . . ) and then I will be cast out of society, and without society (human relationships, running water, sidewalks), I will *die*. That sounds brutal and maybe dramatic, but that's what truly lies at the heart of our fear. That there will exist no place in the world for us if we're not perfect.

So when we're afraid of making a mistake—of showing something that is a work-in-progress or less than perfect—but we *do it anyway*, let's give ourselves credit. We are not just kids at school, or just a junior copywriter at a corporation, or just an executive in the boardroom, we are epic fucking warriors. We are gladiators in the arena facing the biggest fear of them all: death. Every time we talk ourselves into trying something new (even though that opens us up to making a dreaded mistake), we are actually facing that whole running tape of "trying something new means I might make a mistake, means I might get rejected, which means I might be forced out of society, which means I might die." Thus, when we try something new or when we eschew perfectionism, we are *facing our fear of dying*. I mean, how badass is that? Warrior material for sure.

It's important to face this fear head on, because if we do, we live fuller lives. Fuller lives that allow us to share our art, be creative, try new things, make change in the world. Because if we allow ourselves to make mistakes, to make mediocre work and release it, and to keep making new things and new mistakes and new mediocre work, one day we will make something amazing and world-changing. And isn't that what we all want, deep down?

19. Sharon Stone

# CHAPTER 19
# Sharon Stone

## YOU CAN ONLY SLEEP YOUR WAY TO THE MIDDLE.

*—frequently attributed to Sharon Stone*

*I don't know if Sharon Stone actually said this amazing* line, but I'd like to imagine she did, and it went something like this:

**EXT. GRAUMAN'S CHINESE THEATRE—NIGHT**

It is the opening of an amazing, sexy movie. The iconic theater entrance is packed with stars and reporters. SHARON STONE, ageless, in a red halter evening dress glides across the pavement riddled with handprints of famous history-making actors like her. She has just finished the red carpet and is headed toward the theater entrance but the press cannot stop hounding her.

                    REPORTER 1
     Sharon! Who are you wearing?!

                    REPORTER 2
     Sharon! What diet are you on?!

                    REPORTER 3
     Sharon! What do you say to your critics
     who say you slept your way to the top?!

Sharon pauses, mid-glide. She deigns to give
this last question two seconds of her precious,
fabulous life. She doesn't turn around fully,
merely glances back over her perfect shoulder.

                    SHARON STONE
     You can only sleep your way to the
     middle.
And with a hair flip she disappears into the
theater.


This is so BALLER, right? And by the way, I don't care if anyone ever says I slept my way to the top, I'd take it as a compliment. I think in order to get anywhere, the point isn't that you need to have sex or need to not have sex to get to the top but that you have to be a whole person. The assumption that sexuality itself disqualifies a person from merit or value is innately destructive. If you get to the top by squelching any part of yourself, you're not going to be a whole, happy person. It so happens that the thing most often squelched is your joy, femininity, and sexuality. On the other hand, if women get to the top with only their sexuality and squelch their intelligence and creativity they also do not feel whole and happy. If you're at the top and you're not happy, then really, you're only in the middle.

However you get to the top, enjoy it, embrace the totality of you, do things that you can stand by, don't be afraid of mistakes . . .

Which comes to my point: Just like you can only sleep your way to the middle, you can only perfectionist your way to the middle.

We often cling to perfectionism because, well, it promises perfection, and isn't that the very definition of "top." But the great deceit of perfectionism is that it never brings you to the top, it only, at best, brings you to the middle. If you have been relying on perfectionism most of your life and find that you've plateaued, well, it means to get to the next level, you've got to release perfectionism. Many of the most admired thinkers, doers, and creative geniuses of our time are not perfectionists. If you want to be among them, you cannot be a perfectionist either.

When you adopt this philosophy, let it comfort you. When people nitpick at you, or point out your mistakes, and you suddenly feel homesick for your old ways of perfectionism (you might think, ah! Had I only been more of a perfectionist I could have avoided this stinging criticism and embarrassing mistake), remember, perfectionism only takes you to the middle, and you're on your way to the top. And if the people around you don't see that, well, very soon they will!

A rewrite of the scene:

**EXT. GRAUMAN'S CHINESE THEATRE—NIGHT**

                    REPORTER 3
          Krista! What do you say to your critics
          who say you perfectionisted your way to
          the top?!

Krista pauses, mid-glide. She deigns to give this
last question two seconds of her precious, fabu-

lous life. She doesn't turn around fully, merely
glances back over her perfect shoulder.

                    KRISTA SUH
        You can only perfectionist your way to
        the middle.

And with a hair flip she disappears into the
theater.

Okay, so it doesn't have the same ring to it, but I don't care. I'm not trying
to be perfect, because I'm headed to the top!

# CHAPTER 20
## The Worry Dance Is Optional

I share a living space with my brother, and neither of us are particularly neat people. Sure, we try. We keep most of our stuff off the floor. We get most of the dishes done quickly. We get the disinfectant spray out when something looks exceptionally disgusting. But we're not perfect. Every so often he'll come home to find I've littered the sofa with papers. Or I'll find his cereal bowl from the day before on the kitchen table, crusty and gross. You know how it goes. One person's innocent "I'll get that eventually" mess starts to grate on their roommate, who makes a fuss, only to be confronted by evidence of their own misdeeds.

I have had that fight with my brother. Many times.

Eventually, I got to a point where the fight just seemed . . . dumb. Why were we doing this to ourselves? And I proposed a solution. I'd previously hired a housekeeper to tidy the place in the run-up to a few of my parties. She was honest, hardworking, and she seemed eager for a few extra hours. We could hire her to come once a week, and my brother and I would never need to have this stupid, anxiety-making, repetitive fight again.

My brother initially balked at the idea, but I talked him into it. We'd been satisfied with her services in the past. Hiring her was tantamount to creating economic opportunity, which made both of our socially conscious hearts a little warmer. Having this level of support, and paying money for it, was going to make a big difference in the quality of all our lives. Eventually, he agreed. I was about to head off and let her know when he stopped me. He stood in the doorway to his bedroom and yelled, "We should be able to do this ourselves!"

I didn't quite know what to make of this. I was going to launch into a repeat of our discussion and debate until I realized that he wasn't trying to stop me from calling her. We'd already decided that we were definitely on the hiring-a-housekeeper road. He wasn't trying to reopen the negotiation. So what did he want?

Turns out, all he wanted was to tell me this one thing. To communicate this strange artifact of worry and concern. Even though the problem was solved. Even though we weren't going to deviate from this plan. He wasn't trying to change anything—he was just going through extra worry emotions, like he was doing an ancient dance. A Worry Dance.

A Worry Dance is a peculiar ritual we have all done at some time. It makes us feel less foolish later, because if things go wrong, you can point back to the Worry Dance you did and say, "See?! I wasn't a complete idiot. I *knew* this could happen. I even did a Worry Dance about it!"

But it's a strange and paltry reward because the Worry Dance is very taxing on our psyches, emotions, and bodies. What does your body feel like on worry? Not good, right?

There are plenty of worries that can go away if you take a particular action. You can prepare for a nerve-racking test by studying. You can prepare for the nuclear apocalypse by building and stocking a fallout shelter. But there are limits to worry that a lot of people don't seem to recognize. What point is there in worrying about a job interview that you've already had? It's over, and there's no rewind button. Why should you spend any energy worrying about things you have no control over? You can't affect the outcome of a game you're not playing just as you cannot get a horror movie victim to look behind her by shouting at the screen. She will always run up the stairs. There's no stopping her.

In so many of these situations, your anxiety does nothing except create more anxiety. You don't need it. No matter how much you think you do. I used to shame myself over parking tickets. I freaked out over each one and self-flagellated, telling myself what a bad person I was for getting a parking ticket. To ease my anxiety, I made myself a deal—I was allowed one parking ticket every two years. I figured it was a reminder that parking tickets don't make me a bad person, they just happen, and as long as I wasn't getting them all the time, I'd be fine. This worked pretty well until one day I found an even better solution. I was running late for a dinner date and parked my car in a one-hour parking zone. I had such a good time at the dinner, I completely forgot to go out and re-up my meter. When my date walked me to the car, he saw the parking ticket and grabbed it. "I'll take care of it. It's super easy online. Pretend it's not even there," he said. I looked at him, shocked to my core.

Because unbeknownst to him, I had started in on my shame spiral. "Oh my God, you're such a bad person, Krista, how could you, this is a waste of money, had you been a little more careful . . . " and his quick solution to it completely cut off my shame spiral: *I'll pay it and we'll never have to think about it again.* It was a ticket for sixty dollars, and while that was a lot of money for me, I could have paid it without wildly disrupting my life. Yes, it was amazing that he paid it for me and I didn't have to see one dent in my bank balance. But the real gift he'd given me was something I had been denying myself. Absolution. Freedom from the shame spiral.

I realized that my Worry Dance about parking tickets was based on an outdated childish thought: If I worry enough about it, I can prevent it from happening. If I shame myself about it, I will be extra vigilant about it never happening. But the amount of energy I was putting into the Worry Dance didn't really help me in the long run, because the truth is that I didn't *need* the Worry Dance to prevent me from being a crazy devil-may-care parker. In reality, I didn't get very many parking tickets, with or without the shame spiral.

---

**EXERCISE**

## Cutting into the Worry Dance

Can I get you to get to Z without worry?

Examples:

I am worried about my son's ballet recital. If I worry about my son's ballet recital, he will do well and avoid teasing.

Can you get to "My son will do well and avoid teasing" without worry?

You can help him do better at the recital by not worrying (which I'm sure stresses him out) and by helping him make sure he has enough time to practice.

*I am worried about [A].*

*If I worry about [A],*

*I will [Z].*

While you can't control other kids' behavior about teasing, you can talk to your son about loving the performance in his own body, and caring about what *he* thinks, not what other kids think.

You can use that extra time you freed up from Not Worrying by getting a massage for yourself.

---

The Worry Dance is completely optional. You'll be amazed at all the areas you can apply this to. In the lead-up to the Pussyhat Project, I was interviewed by several media outlets. I had never been in front of the camera or the microphone so often. It was a blessing that there were so many of them, because not only did it increase the reach of the Pussyhat Project, the many news outlets prevented me from agonizing over my performance in any one interview (i.e., dancing the Worry Dance). As the interviews aired, I didn't watch my performance, because I didn't need any information from the videos. My job was done. At that point, I knew that if I watched them, I wasn't in a place where I could learn from them. Watching them over and over again would only lead to the Worry Dance.

We treat worry like a strange kick-starter fuel. We believe that if we worry enough, and shame ourselves enough, we will get our engine going and do great things in the world, e.g., if I worry about parking tickets enough, I will save money and be a good citizen (or I can skip the worry and just be a good citizen). If I worry about my interviews enough, I will get better at interviews (or I could just skip the worry and get better at interviews). See what the worry in your life is trying to lead you to . . . and then see if the worry is optional. You'll probably find that it is.

21. You Are Enough,
No More Rubrics

# CHAPTER 21
# You Are Enough, No More Rubrics

My favorite Disney princess movie is Cinderella. I love the artwork, the songs, the magic, the gown, the fact that the prince only has five lines. There's a scene that I think is critical to feminism today, and it's not about the dress or being rescued; it's about moving the goalposts and making women jump through hoops. I'm talking, of course, about the Wicked Stepmother. At first she tells Cinderella *of course* she can go to the ball . . . *if* she finishes all her chores and *if* she finds something suitable to wear. The stepmother and stepsisters then proceed to give Cinderella an overwhelming number of chores, never intending to allow her to go to the ball (even though the invitation is for every eligible maiden in the land!).

As women living in this society, we are told by the patriarchy, "Yes, of course we will accept you, yes, of course you can go to the ball *if you finish* all your chores and *if* you find something suitable to wear—sounds fair, right?" And since we women are a can-do type of people, we wholeheartedly agree to it. The patriarchy then dumps more and more conditions on us. Oh, you missed a button, come help me with my outfit now, wash the dishes, etc. And even if, against all odds, we manage to *do* all the chores and we *do* find something suitable to wear, they end up tearing our dress to shreds anyway and trotting off to the ball without us.

I think of these conditions, these moving goalposts, as rubrics. Instead of saying outright that they don't want us at the ball or in a position of power, they'd rather point to a rubric (of their own making) and say, "Oh, it's not *us* rejecting you, it's you rejecting you. You didn't measure up in the rubric."

And of course, the rubric always changes. That's why a woman can be chastised for being a prude and sniggered at for being a slut. Don't dress like a man, but don't be so overtly sexual, or feminine, or girly, or cute. You need to be assertive in the workplace, but not like that, don't be shrill. Don't be vain and fuss over your looks so much, but don't be so plain and look like you've given up on life, it's really putting a damper on my mood.

The thing is, the men (and women) representatives of the patriarchy say these things, and they think they mean them, but what they might not realize is that deep down, they don't care, they just need any reason to stop you from going to the ball to which you were invited.

I think the pussyhats blare out an unspoken message of "You are enough." Come out now, come join the movement now, you don't need to wait, you are enough *now*. You deserve equality *now*. You don't need to be more assertive or less shrill, you are enough now. You don't need to be more modest or more sexy, you are enough now. Please don't wait until you are x number of pounds to speak up. Please don't wait until you talk with fewer "likes" or without vocal fry or without an accent to speak up. Your sisters need you, and you are enough now.

And another note on this . . . there's this thing called the Suffering Olympics, where the downtrodden compete for attention based on who has suffered more. The patriarchy puts out generous resources for its own interests and limited resources for oppressed groups. In this space of scarce resources (of money, aid, attention, or even acknowledgment) it encourages oppressed peoples to compete with each other. Under the Suffering Olympics, in order to get help, in order to "deserve" help, we feel like we need to show how much we've suffered. All this rather than dismantle the false allocation of limited resources to begin with. And then, here's the rub: even when you do speak up, sometimes you are told you haven't suffered *enough*. Or that the group you are speaking up for has not suffered enough. The message is, "Because of insufficient suffering, you are denied, please come back next year when you have suffered more."

Don't let that trick stop you from speaking up, and speaking your truth. I am here to tell you. You are enough. And that includes this: You have suffered enough.

**EXERCISE**

## How Me Is It?

Next time you're making a decision (which car to buy, which school to go to, which fabulous person to date), instead of asking if your options are good or bad, smart or dumb, right or wrong, ask "How Krista is it?" (If your name is Krista, that is!) Reject societal rubrics, and see how "*you*" the option is. Ask, "How <your first name here> is it?" Instead of asking the patriarchy, "Is this right?" ask yourself, "Is this <your first name here?>" i.e., "is this *me*?"

"I really like your watch"

"I really like you"

22. The Ask

# CHAPTER 22
# The Ask, or, the Fear of Being Demanding

*There are two things I look forward to in life:*

1. *Becoming an old lady and cutting in line.*
2. *Becoming pregnant and having the father of my child run all over the city getting things to satisfy my food cravings.*

The second one I learned about on sitcoms; contemporary ones use the trope, but *I Love Lucy* does it best. Ricky walks into the apartment carrying a takeout bag. Lucy: "Oh, honey, what took you so long?!" Ricky: "What do you mean what took me so long? There's only one store in New York with papaya juice milkshakes." Lucy sips her milkshake and then dips a dill pickle in it, as Ricky looks on in disgust and amazement. *That's going to be me one day*, I thought gleefully.

Then I read a horrifying piece of science journalism that crushed this fantasy and ruined everything for me.

Apparently, science suggests that pregnant women don't have particular cravings during pregnancy; they are just more vocal about them, and men are more invested in answering the cravings during that time.[3]

Mind blown, dreams pulverized. I wanted to be treated like an empress, but I didn't want to feel guilty about *wanting* to be treated like an empress. Instead, I wanted to pass the buck onto pregnancy and the attendant "biological cravings" I assumed were a kind of imperative, and a unique one.

Using biology as the fallback reason for my desires spares me from the embarrassment of *wanting*. Just *wanting*. Without any justification. Without any biological reason. Without any deserving. Just wanting.

Wanting for the sake of wanting can feel very scary. Why? Because society has trained women to be demanding only in very limited instances. We can be demanding during weddings, pregnancy, and in our old-lady-ness. At any other time, such insistence on getting what we want is frowned upon. "Demanding" is also used as pejorative word (and its cousin, "needy"). It's not cool for a woman to be demanding, because it means she's a bitch, domineering, too manly without actually being a man, pushy, unfeminine, the list goes on. All of these words and labels are designed to make us feel bad about having desires, expressing them, and working to fulfill them.

My mom's side of the family comes from a province in China called Hunan. In Hunanese there is a word, "*luo suo,*" that has a very particular meaning. I'll try my best to describe it: it means fussy, demanding, overly picky, annoying. When spoken aloud, the word is often accompanied by eye rolling. It's like if you were at someone's grandma's house and were offered a glass of water, and then you asked for sparkling water and a lime. People would glance at each other and roll their eyes and say, "*Luo suo.*" The word implies that it is not your place to ask for what you really want—to demand it—and that you should simply be grateful for what you have, for what has been given to you.

---

3  Hunt, K. (2015, November 5). "Pregnancy Cravings May Not Be Real." Retrieved from Thrillist: https://www.thrillist.com/eat/nation/what-causes-pregnancy-cravings

The word is often used in an endearing way, but all the same, I learned it as the *worst* thing one could be.

It's not just little Chinese American kids who feel this way. I see it all the time at restaurants, where you're paying to have a meal. There's always a table where the wrong dish arrives for a woman, and her friend is like, "You should say something," and the woman meekly whispers, "It's okay."

I call this the fear of being *luo suo*. You're causing another person some inconvenience, you're being demanding or high maintenance.

I'm not saying that we have to always go around picking apart people's generous offers and demanding that it's our way or the highway, but I've designed a simple test for myself when I experience doubt, and it helps me determine whether to take action and speak up or to let it go. Here are the two questions: "Am I not doing this out of fear of speaking up? Or am I doing this to be a good sport?"

I like the phrase "good sport" because it implies an ownership of one's power. You have the power to speak up for yourself and have things your way, or done the way you want them to be done, or done to your standards—however you want to slice it—but this one time, you're gonna choose to have a little less for yourself so the whole team or the whole game can benefit.

Demanding things for ourselves has always been socially challenging. If you're too demanding, people call you "difficult" or "high maintenance." But standing up for the thing you want is necessary and important work—not just for you, but for everyone. It creates ripples of change.

Asking may be one of the most terrifying things we have to do, and it can be a particularly nasty trap for women. The sheer act of asking can feel like an admission to some embarrassing truth: that we need help (well, everyone does), or that we are "lesser" (nope).

Asking opens us up to rejection. It reveals what we want, and this can feel overly intimate, too close. The logic might go like this: if we're asking for what we want, then we ARE the ask, and if people reject what we're asking for, then they are rejecting US. See how that works? Only it DOESN'T work, it just makes us terrified of asking. And if you don't ask, you will not receive.

And if we are rejected, we might feel that we will be deemed unworthy *forever*. We might remember the shame of asking and not receiving, and never ask for anything we want or need again. And if we deem ourselves unworthy, or crazy, or demanding, we might be cast out of society, and then, we might *die*—from loneliness, starvation, and lack of sidewalks, running water, and cable television.

I mean, that's how I felt anyway. That was the depressing end point of this logic stream.

It also doesn't help that it seems that the work or task of asking is so much harder for a woman than it is for a man. When a woman asks for something, there seems to be a strong sense within society of "How dare you ask me to give you something I can't give? How dare you put me in this uncomfortable position?"

One day, I was walking home from the farmer's market, minding my own business, when I saw the Most Beautiful Man. Tall, blond hair, green eyes. He was in a T-shirt with a nonprofit logo on it and guarding a sculpture the nonprofit was putting up as a temporary public art piece.

And because I was confident (it was a confident day during a confident week), I went right up to him and asked, "Are you *guarding* this statue?" It was flirtatious, I admit.

We chatted, and it dawned on me that this Perfect Male Specimen was flirting BACK at me. We were co-flirting, in it together, it was ON. And this was too much for me. I started freaking out, looking for the nearest exit.

"I really like your watch," he said, indicating my Kate Spade watch, with its multicolored watch face. (It really is an awesome watch.)

And instead of doing the smart thing, like amping up our sexual chemistry, I dampened the whole thing by going on a long meaningless tirade. "Oh, this watch? Yeah, I was going to get another one, but then—" I saw his eyes glaze over, and the flirt vibe was kaput.

And then I said I had to go, and left, or rather, scurried away.

I mean, we all know what "I really like your watch" means, right? I really like your watch means I really like you! I *knew* this. The primal, smart, and intuitive part of me could HEAR "I like you" as plain as day.

So why did I screw up my chance to be with, or at least get to know, this Most Beautiful Man?

I was twenty-eight at the time, and after some experiences positive, negative, and in between, I felt pretty confident around men. But this experience made me realize that I was only confident if I thought I had the upper hand. On that day, I had a disturbing realization: there's a difference between going after what you want, and going after what you think you can get. I thought I was pretty good at flirting, but really, I was building up the illusion of confidence by only sticking with guys I thought would be interested, or that I knew were already interested, and in that way, were low hanging fruit on the Tree of Flirt. The Most Beautiful Man was someone I wanted, but not someone I thought I could get, so I ran for the flirt-free hills.

Shortly after I had this realization, I knew that I wanted to change my ways. How sad would it be if I stayed in my comfort zone, and only went after what I thought I could get? Even if I threw my net a bit wider, there would be plenty of times where I'd want something and would ignore that nagging desire in order to avoid uncertainty and the potential sting of rejection.

My life coach, Lauren, who has been helping me for four years with my career and relationships, assigned me a TED Talk by Jia Jiang called "What I Learned from 100 Days of Rejection." A man realizes that he is getting in his own way, and is not able to achieve his full potential because he's too afraid of rejection. He doesn't grow because he doesn't take risks. One day he decides to get over his fear by seeking out a rejection a day for 100 days until he is desensitized to its sting.

Lauren asked me to seek out three rejections before our next Skype session.

I'll just tell you about the rejection that stung the most. I was at a party with my friend, I didn't know anybody else in attendance, and I was dressed

EXERCISE

## People Say Yes to Me

"People say yes to me"—say it hundreds of times, as needed.

"People say yes to me"—write it, hundreds of times, as needed.

"People say yes to me"—think it, arm yourself with it, each time you start a new ask.

I used to walk around with this belief: people say no to me. When I received a no, I would add this as another piece of evidence to the treatise "people say no to me." This overriding thought made me shrug off the times people *did* say yes to me as a fluke, and I hardly remembered them because I wasn't keeping a list of times "people said yes to me," I was so busy with the "no" list. One day, I realized that I had to change this thought because it was making me an anxious, deluded mess.

   I introduced a new belief, a mantra: People say *yes* to me. As you can imagine, since I had been believing the opposite for so long, I had to repeat the mantra "people say yes to me" many times before it could take hold and replace the old belief. But it worked. Now I go around thinking *people say yes to me*, and if I get a no, I shrug that off as a fluke. I have so many instances and stories and memories of people saying "yes!" to me now! Notice that it doesn't even matter how many yeses and how many nos I'm getting. Neither "people say no to me" NOR "people say yes to me" is correct 100 percent of the time, but which one serves me more? By far, the winner of this bout is "people say yes to me." When I have that as my operating thought, when I enter a situation with an ask, I am confident and glowing with excitement, eager to share why the person I'm talking to will LOVE saying yes. I'm not entering the situation steeling myself for a "no." It's an amazing little trick that WORKS!

to the nines, in my skintight, beige minidress with white lace on top—creating the effect that I was only wearing a thin layer of lace. I felt scandalous and sexy. People from the film and TV industry were milling about and schmoozing, including some dancers from the *Step Up* movies. One of them was super-tall and handsome, and I tried to linger near him and encourage him to come talk to me. He didn't make a move, and with Lauren's instructions in my head, I thought to myself, *Okay, you have to talk to him*. I was determined to overcome the fear of going after what I wanted, regardless of rejection. I didn't want to limit myself for the rest of my life, only going after what I knew I could get.

I talked to him and flirted with him, and soon it became clear that he was married, that his hot wife was standing right next to him, and that they had a child at home.

I was mortified.

"Haha, okay, byeeeeeee," is the last thing I remember saying to them.

But as I drove my giggly drunk friend home that night, and went over the interaction in my head, I realized that this rejection was a success, not just because I had completed my homework for my life coach, but because had I *not* gone for it, had I *not* experienced rejection, I would be in a different mood in the car. Instead of sitting in a moment of reflection, I would be in Yearning Mode. I would be attached to an entire narrative (and in this case, it would have been false), assuming that this guy was wonderful and witty and wealthy and powerful and oh-so-handsome and available and would probably—no, *definitely*—be the perfect boyfriend for me if only he knew to talk to me. Instead I talked to him and he proved to be not only unavailable, but also not so witty and probably not that well-off. I'm not saying this to diminish him but merely to point out that by actually *interacting* with him, it humanized him, made him real and not just a fantasy. I was in the car, firmly in the present moment, not yearning for a projection of my own desires. I thought: this is such a powerful and more fulfilling way for me to live!

So ask! Ask, and if rejected, live to ask another day, grateful that you are not stuck in yearning and uncertainty.

# CHAPTER 23
# Is Your Ask Viral?

Every day I get hundreds of emails from people across the country and across the world who are in awe of the Pussyhat Project and want to know how I started a movement. I think of it not as starting a movement but initiating a viral ask.

That's right: a movement is nothing more than a viral ask.

Let me unpack what I mean by "viral ask." A funny YouTube video about cats chasing a blinking light across the wall that goes viral, but doesn't ask you to answer a call for action—social, political, personal, or otherwise—is not a movement. An ask that stops at just one person is not a movement, but if that person you ask then asks other people, who then in turn ask others, then it keeps going—suddenly your ask is a movement.

"Pitching" is a word that is often used in the entertainment industry. Gradually I came to understand that pitching is like asking but with more showmanship. Now I use the word all the time. Pitching in television means presenting the idea for a show and asking someone to buy into the story and finance it to make it into an actual series (for millions of dollars, so you know, no big deal).

In the television industry you're told that when you pitch a new show, you're not just pitching to people in that room. As the creator you must COMMUNICATE your pitch in such a way that the person can then pitch it to the higher-ups, the people who will pony up the money for your project to be made. The concept and methodology of the ask is not just for interpersonal situations, but in business and career situations as well. In this case, can you communicate *your* ask in such a way that the person you've asked can easily ask another? (Your ask becomes their ask.) Can you "arm" the person you're pitching to with the words and language and enthusiasm so they can go to the next person and pitch on your behalf? Will that language and enthusiasm carry over so that the new person being asked is won over and can then go to his or her higher-up and do it again? Are you teaching HOW to ask another in your ask itself so once that person says yes, they are inherently trained to get a yes from someone else? As you can see, it's like a domino effect. The key is asking in the correct way so that all the dominos fall together and at the right time.

For the Pussyhat Project, I wrote a manifesto and a core team worked together to make the "ask" as clear and easy and poignant and shareable as possible. Kat, a local knitting store owner, became our knit pattern designer and made the hat pattern as easy and affordable as possible. Jayna, a fellow knitting enthusiast, became a co-founder and was a big proponent in making the pick-up and drop-off points for hats as easy as possible. Aurora, an artist I knew through a friend, made the artwork for the social media sites beautiful and shareable. In my manifesto I aimed to give people the words and philosophy that would allow them to easily promote the project and, if necessary, defend the project to the people they spoke to.

## A Note on Ease and Difficulty

Oddly enough, sometimes when you make things too easy for people, they are inclined to say no. In the end, we all crave a challenge—not one that is out of our reach, but a challenge that we have to work for just a bit.

Although we're always going on about wanting a free lunch, the reality is that we don't cherish what we don't work for in the same way as we value something we DO work for. The necessity of work and challenge creates just the right amount of friction so that people feel like they are doing something with purpose. And we all crave purpose.

When I was campaigning for Hillary in Ohio, I went on my first canvassing trip to promote early voting. It was then I noticed that early voting is a conundrum—it is more convenient and the lines are shorter, but people also feel like they don't get the "pomp and circumstance" of going on election day to vote, maybe waiting in lines, even, or feeling a part of something, feeling as though they had to put forth an effort to equal an outcome. But if the lines on election day are *too* long then people gripe and sometimes give up and don't vote at all. It's finding that happy medium of a doable challenge.

The pussyhat had to be easy enough for people to give it a try, but if it was too easy, people wouldn't feel like they were really doing something meaningful, or that they were part of a movement, which the Pussyhat Project quickly became. Challenge adds meaning and purpose, which will inevitably draw people in, and those people will ask others to be involved, and so on and so forth. And in this way, movements are born.

24. Reciprocity and the Gift of Epic

# CHAPTER 24
# Reciprocity and the Gift of Epic

What stops so many of us from engaging in the art of the ask or even considering the possibility is that we often mistakenly assume that everything has to be reciprocal. We're afraid that what we have to offer is not enough to equal the effort or time or money that we're asking for in exchange.

First of all, what kind of blows my mind to this day—even though I've seen evidence of it daily—is that *people like to help*. For example, most New Yorkers secretly love being asked for directions by tourists even though they complain about it. Bottom line, people like to help. It doesn't feel reciprocal, but sometimes, what you're offering in return is the *opportunity to help* and that's it, and sometimes that's enough. People feel good about helping. It's a primal urge, and movements can utilize that to everyone's advantage.

It's helpful to think of what's known as the Ben Franklin effect. In reciprocity, you would assume that if you want a favor from someone, you should offer to do a favor for them. The Ben Franklin effect turns this on its head by saying no, you don't offer to do a favor for them, you ask them for a small doable favor *from* them to get you in the door, and then follow up with the bigger favor later.

In his autobiography, Franklin explains how he won over another legislator using his trademark particular technique:

"Having heard that he had in his library a certain very scarce and curious book, I wrote a note to him, expressing my desire of perusing that book, and requesting he would do me the favour of lending it to me for a few days. He sent it immediately, and I return'd it in about a week with another note, expressing strongly my sense of the favour. When we next met in the House, he spoke to me (which he had never done before), and with great civility; and he ever after manifested a readiness to serve me on all occasions, so that we became great friends, and our friendship continued to his death."[4]

The thing about asking is this: sometimes you aren't the best judge of what constitutes reciprocity or an equitable exchange. It's helpful to realize that it's not always about total equality, and that even determining a metric for measurement is itself an imperfect process. For example, sometimes you're asking for something concrete and what you're offering back is something abstract: like the chance to help. When I first moved to Hollywood, I underestimated the value of my youth. A lot of people took meetings with me simply because they wanted to know what the young people were thinking, or they wanted to be around youthful energy and feel young again themselves. I didn't know that when I was twenty-two, and I try to delicately tell that to young people who are just starting out in the business. It's helpful to see what you bring to the table—to expand your understanding of what that might be—and be open to the idea that what you're offering "in return" is more abstract.

Another example of something valuable, yet abstract, that you might be offering in return is the Gift of Epic.

4  Independence Hall Association. (2017). *Page 48*. Retrieved from The Electric Ben Franklin: http://www.ushistory.org/franklin/autobiography/page48.htm

I firmly believe that if the needs for food, water, and shelter are met, the next thing all human beings NEED is the feeling of EPIC. We want to be heroines. We want to feel like our lives have meaning and purpose. We want the opportunity to be a part of making history.

When I designed the Pussyhat Project, I knew I wanted people to be a part of a story we would write together. A story in which EVERYONE was a hero or heroine with an EPIC storyline. The marchers were epic. The knitters were epic. Engaging with and OWNING the epic gives your life meaning and purpose and grandeur. And when you're offering that, whatever you're asking for (money, support, a website, a service) seems small and easy in comparison. So what's your ideal epic? And how could you offer the epic to someone else?

I once tried to ask a woman who had worked on the television show *Friends* to mentor me in screenwriting, and I racked my brain for what I could offer her in return. Did she have kids? Free babysitting? Did she need someone to take notes for her, to pick up dry cleaning? This dilemma really freaked me out, and I lost my nerve. Now that a few years have passed, I realize that my mentors don't NEED anything from me—they don't need me to pick up their dry cleaning or babysit. If anything they NEED my youth or my happiness or my charm or my fervor or my determination, because it gives them the feeling of meaning, purpose, unadulterated joy, intensity of life. In short, it gives them the EPIC. When you're just starting out in a new industry it can be difficult to realize what you are bringing to the table, what your very unique gifts are, the epic you offer, but once you know (and sometimes these things are more ethereal), you can feel more solid and confident in your ask.

And having said all that, you can also ask without offering anything in return!

25. Fear of Rejection Comes From
Fear of Rejecting.

# CHAPTER 25
# Fear of Rejection Comes from Fear of Rejecting

## 1. Fear of Rejection Comes from Fear of Rejecting

It's hard to ask a question that might be met with a no if you are afraid of saying no to other people. If saying no gives you so much trouble, then of course you'll feel bad asking somebody for something and then "making" them feel bad for saying no. The reality is, you're not making them do anything. "No" is respectful, clear, and to the point.

The fear of asking and being rejected stems directly from our own anxieties about saying no. Just no. Without qualifications or apologies. Think about it: if you're afraid of saying no, afraid of how people are going to view you if you say no to any request no matter how small, and maybe even how you'll view yourself if you say no, then when it's *your* turn to ask someone to do anything similar, you might project *your* anxieties about saying no on to them. Then, when that person says no, you'll feel as though you've put them through some kind of anguish, which actually might or might not be too far from the truth. See how exhausting that is? If we could eliminate anxiety and anguish around saying no, this would be no problem at all!

## 2. Don't Date an Amusement Park Sign!

I once dated a gorgeous man with blond hair and blue eyes who was well over six feet tall, had been an army paratrooper, spoke and wrote Chinese fluently, and founded a socially conscious company that helped educate young kids in underserved areas.

I KNOW. This description, on paper, screams THIS IS THE PERFECT MAN FOR ME.

But he wasn't. Because when I was completely, brutally honest with myself, I wasn't in love with him as much as the *idea* of him. As I gave this more consideration, it occurred to me that I enjoyed going out with him, enjoyed the experience of being on his arm because I was hoping that he would protect me from the potential attentions of other men.

He was like an amusement park sign that said, "You must be THIS tall to ride this ride." "You must be THIS handsome to date Krista, you must be this wealthy to approach Krista, you must be this successful to even *look* at Krista." Subconsciously, I was hoping that he would protect me from having to interact with guys I didn't want to date, i.e., I was hoping that he would save me from the ordeal of having to say "no."

Many of us have done some version of this in some part of our lives. We've gone through all sorts of trouble and

EXERCISE

## Practice saying no to THREE people without apologies or justification.

If that's too hard, you can start off with a go-to reason and slowly wean yourself off of justification.

For example:

> No, I need time for my main priorities X, Y, and Z, and I don't want to say yes when I cannot properly prioritize it and give you the experience you deserve. I hope you find someone awesome who is a better fit for you. Maybe you can ask Person A—she is someone I recommend.

Next, say no without giving a recommendation:

> No, I need time for my main priorities X, Y, and Z, and I don't want to say yes when I cannot properly prioritize it and give you the experience you deserve. ~~I hope you find someone awesome who is a better fit for you. Maybe you can ask Person A—she is someone I recommend.~~

Next, say no without naming your priorities:

> No, I need time for my main priorities ~~x, y, and z,~~ and I don't want to say yes when I cannot properly prioritize it and give you the experience you deserve. ~~I hope you find someone awesome who is a better fit for you. Maybe you can ask Person A—she is someone I recommend.~~

Eventually, you might get to a "no" like this:

> No, thank you.

And eventually, perhaps your no will look like:

> No.

jumped through all sorts of hoops to save ourselves the grief of having to say "no." I had a friend in college who would suddenly fall ill before an event she didn't want to attend because she couldn't bear to say no; it was easier to be sick, and it was also an acceptable excuse.

When you say no, you are facing the fear of being labeled a demanding, unaccommodating, crazy woman. The first few times it might feel uncomfortable, even borderline unbearable, but over time, it will get increasingly easier. And getting to a place where saying no to events, people, situations, ideas, jobs, etc., that DON'T serve you is worth it. Your whole life becomes more enjoyable, more fulfilling. In short, this small change can make you much happier.

**EXERCISE**

## A trick for saying "no" on behalf of your future self

Sometimes, you might get an invitation or opportunity that is far off in the future, maybe even a year from now. It can be tempting to say yes because saying no is hard and it's so far off in the future anyway, you'll cross that bridge when you come to it.

Next time you run into that situation, pretend the event is in two weeks—would you still say yes? If so, reply yes! If not, reply no!

26. GROW Your Garden
of Friends

# CHAPTER 26
# Grow Your Garden of Friends

Cultivating female friendships is one of the best things you can do for yourself. I used to feel really lonely in Los Angeles, but now that I have nurtured my female friendships for several years, I have people to call, people to ask for help, people to get conversation, a consultation, a consolation, or simply just a hug from. These friendships have encouraged me to ask for what I want, in career, romance, and other aspects of my life.

One way to deepen your existing friendships is to state your desires in front of each other. Basically, you are ASKING the universe for what you want and they are witnessing it.

To open up in front of friends, especially with a new friend group, I like to present an exercise I learned from Mama Gena's blog about female empowerment called the Holy Trinity. I also use it as a solo journaling exercise, but it intensifies in power exponentially when you do it with friends.

## Holy Trinity

Stand or sit in a circle (you can hold hands if you want to feel extra committed!) and go around, each person taking a turn. When it's your turn you say:

"I brag that . . . <something you are proud of>" followed by
"I am grateful for <something you are grateful for>" and
"I desire . . . <something you want>."

Once you state your desire, the entire circle of women say, together at the same time, "And so it shall be or something better."

When you express your desires in front of other people and they don't laugh at you or say, "Eh, that would be nice, but how is that ever gonna happen?" but instead nod vigorously and say they *see it happening for you,* that is powerful. That's support and empowerment in female numbers.

Especially when your friends are busy and you don't get to see them that often, the Holy Trinity is an amazing way to get a litmus test of what's going on in their lives at the moment. It brings you to the heart of that person quickly and meaningfully, by eliminating small talk. I've done the Holy Trinity in dance classes and in hotel lobbies, on the phone, in text messages, and on the beach under a new moon. I've done it in a sports bar with men too (and I made those five guys hold hands). It's FANTASTIC. If you're feeling shy, it's really great to do as a journal exercise until you feel ready to do it with a friend. Try it. I guarantee you'll be surprised by the results.

DDIY (Don't Do It Yourself) + Identity

# CHAPTER 27
# DDIY (Don't Do It Yourself) + Identity

When I was twenty-three, I racked up three really expensive speeding tickets in the space of a year. It was mortifying. I'd always thought of myself as an excellent driver, someone with flair and catlike reflexes, someone who got where they were going more quickly and more efficiently than anyone else. I had bought into this cultural understanding of speedy driving as being the sort of thing that marked you as capable and sexy. Action heroes sped. Secret agents sped. I was such a good girl in all aspects of my life, this was the one area where I was exciting and wild. It was part of my identity: *Krista is really square, really solid, really responsible . . . but wow, she's such a sexy driver—speed, prowess, everything.*

The tickets were a bucket of cold water. I knew I had to slow down to stop getting tickets, and yet the second ticket came, and then the third. I would be on the sparsely trafficked freeway at night, resolving to stay at the speed limit, and yet a few exits in, I was passing cars without thought.

I couldn't seem to stop, until I realized that I had to make the change on an identity level. I had to ditch the dangerous idea that speeding was sexy and replace it with a better, healthier ideal. I had a belief, deeply ingrained in me: "I am a great driver. I am fast and I get to places before everyone else." To counteract that, I started saying the following about myself: "I am a safe driver. I drive the speed limit and get to places safely and comfortably. I am a good driver." Like magic, the speeding—and the tickets—stopped coming.

That experience taught me that when desired changes aren't happening on the surface level, it often means we need to dive down deep to the identity level and make adjustments there. Our identity, what we believe to be true of ourselves, is what creates friction. If you run into a problem that causes you more stress than it needs to, it's likely that there's something about your identity that is preventing a peaceful resolution. For example, I was with my mom and my aunt in Toronto for a family wedding. We took the opportunity to explore the city, and at some point during the day, my aunt realized she had lost her wallet. So we retraced our steps, and she was fretting the whole time. No, more than fretting; she was self-flagellating. "Oh my God, this isn't like me, I *never* do this. I *never* lose things, especially my wallet. It's been five minutes, do you think I should cancel my credit cards now?" My mom and I were wide-eyed in wonderment, and couldn't quite relate to her level of angst, because, well, we lose things all the time. I once lost my birth certificate, and my mom produced another one saying that at my birth, she figured her daughter might be like her and lose things, so she got two certificates just in case. "I never lose anything" was *not* a part of our identities, so when we lose things, it's inconvenient but not an existential crisis of "Who am I?" like it was for my aunt. My aunt was afraid that she'd made herself vulnerable by leaving her wallet somewhere in public, and that by doing so, she'd taken leave of her longstanding "vigilant person" identity. That she'd lost control of her belongings and thereby herself. That she'd become *scatterbrained*. She needn't have worried—she hadn't lost her wallet as we traipsed around the city; her wallet had fallen out of her purse and slipped into a crevice of the rental car, and we found it later that day.

Many problems in our day-to-day lives can be traced back to an identity crisis. A major example is the identity myth that "I do things myself" or "I am independent" or "I don't need help." This belief can be inconvenient, and at worst, harmful. So many women are mired in this belief that to be strong they need to do things themselves, and to that I say, "DDIY!" as in, "Don't Do It Yourself!"

Bringing in help can fast-track a project and remove unnecessary suffering. Can you imagine all the things you can accomplish in this world, *for* this world, if you DDIYed and released the identity of "I do things myself?"

There are times when a DIY (do-it-yourself) mind-set is meaningful. You learn something, you feel huge satisfaction at the completion of a task, you revel in the doing of it. But all other times, when you are DIYing and it sucks, consider whether you are resisting help simply out of a need to feed your ego and to cling to a part of your identity that you do not need. If that's the *only* reason you are DIYing a project, I urge you to experiment and call in help. The Pussyhat Project was a "DIY" project that I did *not* do myself—literally millions of women took part. Let your identity beliefs hang looser and see what you can accomplish and how you feel.

It's fun!

A Valentine!
From the Goat
to the Horse

# 28. The Horse and the Goat

## CHAPTER 28
# The Horse and the Goat

There was a thoroughbred racing horse that got very skittish staying in unfamiliar surroundings overnight, such as when it was transported to a race. The next day, it wouldn't perform as well due to lack of sleep. Owners and trainers tried everything, even sedating the horse during transport, but this too affected the race performance, as it was too sluggish. Eventually they found a very easy, incredibly low-tech solution that solved the problem: put a goat in the stall with the horse. The goat was from the horse's home farm and would munch hay alongside the horse during the night. The horse would see the goat chilling, and figure there's nothing to worry about, munch some hay alongside this familiar friend from the farm, and then get a good night's rest before the next day's big race.

Although I'm not a horse enthusiast, this story stayed with me. There was something about it—the notion of a familiar companion reducing anxiety and stress—that clung to me, floating up to the surface of my mind more often than you might think, considering I don't work with horses or goats and have limited experience on farms. I found it helpful and comforting.

And then one day it hit me—this factoid is a metaphor for how I live my life. Whenever I'm in a new situation I ask myself, "Am I the horse or the goat?"

There are times in your life when you will be the one about to race, the one of which much is expected, the one everyone is watching. And there are times when you will be the one meant to support someone about to race with your presence and your companionship. If you can get clear on which role you are to play in each situation, you can do your job beautifully and feel proud of yourself when you're done. In either scenario—racing or supporting, horsing or goating—it's possible to feel accomplished and successful. In other words, sometimes you're the star, and sometimes you're the backup that makes stardom possible.

My friendships improved once I understood this relationship and put it into action. I love to goat my friends. When MILCK was doing her first major photo shoot, she'd somehow gotten a respected photographer—someone with an incredible resume and clients a mile long—to do her a huge favor and take these amazing pictures. I saw her getting ready, and as she was running through her list of things to do—everything from choosing her outfits to buying paint and egg whites for the photo shoot, I was horrified.

"You need an assistant," I told her.

"I think I can handle it," she said. But her face betrayed otherwise—she was nervous.

I told her, "I'm going to be there that day. You have me for the whole day, whatever you want me to do." I didn't say, "I'll goat you," but that's what I was thinking.

The beauty of being a goat is that you get to go into Extreme Helper Mode. I love going to extremes because it makes me feel like an epic warrior. And what's great is that you limit that extreme behavior to a specified time block, e.g., the day of the photo shoot. That way, you won't feel overwhelmed or overtaxed. Instead, you've spent one day or one hour or one

afternoon being a goat, helping to support another person's dreams. Goating means empowering another.

The day of the photo shoot, I sorted through her clothes, laid out options, charged her phones, played music she requested, made and put up inspirational key word signs around the garage we were shooting in, went out to buy the egg whites to thin out paint, laid out plastic for her to walk on while dripping with paint, climbed a short ladder to pour the paint on my naked friend, and then walked her carefully to the shower. At the end of the day, I felt satisfied, and my friend felt successful. It was a win-win.

Whether it's with a friend or a romantic partner, it's important to have a good balance of horsing and goating. I love goating my friends, and part of the reason is because I feel their reciprocity. When I had *my* first photo shoot, MILCK offered to be my assistant for the day. I was horse, and she was goat. She drove me, carried all my clothes, styled me with accessories, cheerlead-ed me through the different shots, kept an eye out for flyaways in my hair, and charmed the photographer, which I think led to even better shots. I felt completely taken care of and relaxed being on the other end of this relationship. I loved the photos and I think I was able to be such a good horse and perform because she was such a good goat.

I'd been horsing and goating long before I had a name for it, because that's how my family operates. If my dad was studying for the medical boards, or if I was studying for a test, or if my brother was training for the Los Angeles Police Department, that person was the horse, the rest of us were goats. I was excused from all family events and dinners so I could study. When my brother applied to the LAPD, I drove him to all his appointments so he could have one less thing to worry about (finding the place, finding parking, etc.). I was dating a guy named Dennis at the time, and I had to leave him in the middle of the night because I was driving my brother in the morning. "Why are you doing that?" he asked as I was leaving. "Why can't he just drive himself?" I didn't know how to answer him; it never occurred to me that not everyone operates like we do. I would have told him about the horse and the goat, but I didn't have those words yet. If anything, I suddenly felt really weird. Why didn't he drive himself? Why was I such a weirdo? But with time, I realized that I wasn't weird at all, I was just practicing a different kind of relationship.

Not everyone will be able to goat you, or even wrap their head around the concept. I dated a guy we'll call Armand for two years and during that time I came up with this language for how I operate. Horse. Goat. He didn't get it; he didn't *like* it. I loved dropping everything to help him with an art project—but this made him uncomfortable. And he didn't feel right doing the same for me. When I explained my horse-goat metaphor he said, "I don't think either of us should sublimate ourselves for the other."

I think this is a huge reason why Armand and I didn't work out. I love living this way, I love sublimating myself for a moment—it doesn't have to be a negative thing, but an empowering thing. I love being *all in* with the sole purpose of supporting another person, and then coming up for air and switching places for a bit or just chilling for awhile. (Sometimes, nobody has to be a horse or a goat. Instead, we can just be any animal we like, kicking back in the fields, having a snack, and enjoying the sunshine.)

If you've never done it, I highly recommend trying it with your friends. Tell them directly that you want to test it. "Let's try horsing and goating each other!" For those of you who help TOO much, this might be a good chance to claim your horse days (where you run the race and get to be the star), and to limit your goat days to specified times. For instance, when my friend Elizabeth mentioned she was moving houses on her birthday a few Augusts ago, I immediately penciled in a goat day—I knew she would be under a lot of stress on a day that was supposed to be special.

During the lead-up to the Women's March, I spent a week in DC preparing logistics and taking interviews from press all over the world. I knew that I would need to horse at my best, and I asked my friends to goat me as best they could. Stefanie found me a local hair and makeup artist and communicated with volunteers; Liz handled all the scheduling of the press; DC neighbors cooked food, baked cookies, and packaged pussyhats into waterproof bags.

Have you ever dreamed of having an assistant? To that, I say, "Dream on!" No, really, dream about it, in distinct detail. Don't just treat it like a passing fantasy. Really think about what having an assistant would look like. It doesn't matter if you actually get one or not, the *thinking* about getting an assistant can be helpful in clarifying situations or tasks that could use some goating by a friend.

---

**EXERCISE**

## Ideal Assistant

Write a manual for the assistant you would hire. Tell her or him about yourself and how you work. Tell them what you need done now, and what you anticipate needing them to do over a one-year period. I LOVE doing this exercise—it makes me take stock of my systems, and explaining them to another (fictional) person is illuminating.

The perfect assistant is...   SMART! THOROUGH! CAPABLE! QUICK! TRUSTWORTHY! FRIENDLY! NO-NONSENSE!

As you do this, imagine that this is the BEST ASSISTANT in the world. She or he is smart, capable, trustworthy, quick, thorough, friendly, and no-nonsense. They can watch your kid, be trusted with access to your bank accounts and all your passwords, make pickups and deliveries, clean, organize, etc.

Now . . . as you blissfully imagine this benevolent presence in your life, write a list of things you CANNOT give this assistant to do. No matter how smart, capable, trustworthy, quick, and thorough they are. This is my list.

*Things I Can't Have an Assistant Do:*

- Have sex, sexy time, or make out with my lover
- Go to a friend's event to support that friend
- Spend time with my family in my place
- Network for me
- Write my novel
- Write my screenplays
- Sleep for me
- Eat for me

- Receive a massage
- Meditate for me
- Work out
- Complete my beauty rituals
- Shower for me
- Get my wax
- Get my manicure
- Get my pedicure
- Get my photo taken

As you come up with a list of things you can have an assistant do, also come up with a list of things you cannot have an assistant do. My list of things I cannot have an assistant do really surprised me. I often let things like sleeping, eating, and working out go by the wayside in favor of "more important things," but isn't the important stuff what you cannot delegate?

When I jotted down this list for the first time, an "ah-ha" moment hit me, and I hope it does for you too. If I sent an assistant to my friend's concert to "support her," that would totally miss the point. I can have my assistant research day spas and make an appointment for me at a spa, but I can't have her receive the massage for me. Nobody can eat or sleep for you. Nope.

Now I prioritize the stuff I can't have an assistant do. Making out. Sleeping. Eating. Showering. Getting a mani-pedi. Spending time with my grandmother. Because there are some things in life you cannot delegate, and these are often the things that make life the most meaningful. I hope and wish that eventually your life will become ONLY about the things that give you joy, and that you delegate the rest of the stuff as needed or wanted.

And I hope you try out the horse-goat scenario, even if you only try it once. After all, we could always, all of us, use a little help from our friends.

29. Mentorship Without Consent

# CHAPTER 29
# Mentorship Without Consent

*I believe there are two types of mentoring:* passive mentorship where the mentor goes about her day and the mentee benefits from observation; and active mentorship where the mentor delves into the mentee's life and gives customized advice.

I used to think that passive mentorship didn't count because I had fantasies of active mentorship. I imagined a powerful mentor would lay eyes on me and pluck me out of the crowd. The mentor would say something like, "*She* is the one, the chosen one."

This didn't really happen to me; in fact, my first active mentor was someone I harangued until she gave in, which is maybe the direct opposite of someone picking you out of a crowd of people and saying, "You." Her name is Nancy Conyers, and she'd be the first to say that she didn't really want to teach me to be a better writer, but that I pestered her and pestered her. I simply wouldn't give up. I had plucked HER out as a mentor, and I was going to have her.

Nowadays, Nancy is not only my mentor but my friend, and she delights in telling the story of how we met. "Krista comes up to me after my reading and said, 'Ms. Conyers, I'd like to take writing lessons from you.'" I don't remember calling her "Ms. Conyers," but Nancy will never forget. Our mentor-mentee "courtship" proceeded as such: She said she didn't have any openings in her classes, I asked if she gave private lessons. She said she wasn't really giving private lessons right now as she was working on her novel. I asked how much she charged. She threw out a number she thought I would balk at. I said sure!

The fact that I was willing to pay for mentorship shows that I was ready to leave behind my fantasy of waiting around to be the "chosen one," and was ready for practical help on my writing.

Nancy is an example of someone who passively *and* actively mentors me. I learn just by observing her—she makes decisions confidently, she handles money well, and she networks with gusto. I see this as passive mentorship because she doesn't have to put in a lot of time and effort into it; she's just being herself and giving me a window into her life. She also actively mentors me. For example, I'll approach her with a problem and she'll listen and offer advice. When she was going through breast cancer and everyone was treading carefully around her, I was probably the only person who was like, "Help me with my problems!" Full disclosure: I made it super clear that I was fully willing to drop it if she wasn't up for it, but it turns out she was. "This is entertaining," she said. Mentorship can be fun for the mentor; it's like the mentee is offering a puzzle or a riddle that the mentor can figure out. It can be entertainment and it can be fulfilling.

Passive mentorship doesn't need consent. That sounds a bit stalker-y, but you can be inspired by someone with or without their permission. People with a public profile are offering passive mentorship opportunities all of the time with their Instagram accounts, Twitter feeds, blogs, interviews, TED talks, etc. I was very inspired by the way Hillary Clinton handled criticism and misogyny throughout her campaign. Many accomplished people have written books or do panel discussions about their process.

I once listened to an interview with Steve Levitan, the head writer of *Modern Family*, speaking about his experiences in the TV business. I was inspired by the way he talked about a failed show—apparently, he had taken the notes from the network and studio, even though he didn't agree with them. The show was cancelled anyway soon after, and he said to himself, "Never again." If he was going to be cancelled, he'd rather it be because of his own mistakes and based on a show he created, not on a show he had compromised on to the point it didn't feel like his anymore. Now when I make decisions on whether to incorporate someone's advice in my own life, I remember that it might not work out anyway, and if that were to happen, would I have been happier doing things my way?

Julia Cameron is the author of *The Artist's Way*, one of the most influential books about engaging with the creative process. She points out that mentors don't even have to be alive—you can read bios of them, be inspired, and think of how your understanding of this person, that vision you hold, would respond to the questions you have. Elizabeth Taylor is my example of a person who passively mentored me when press started rising up for the Pussyhat Project. I've always seen her as fearless and bold: a woman who completely owned her sexuality and was unashamed of it, and also she was a star who was a bit mischievous with the press. I've never met her, and of course I never will, but she is my passive mentor nonetheless.

30. How to Talk to Rich People

# CHAPTER 30
# How to Talk to Rich People

Wealth manifests in a variety of ways, some of which have nothing to do with the green stuff. A rich person *can* be wealthy in money (maybe they can invest in your idea), but they might also be wealthy in powerful connections (maybe they can introduce you to the right people); or wealthy in popularity (maybe they can tweet your business to their millions of followers, or let you sit at the cool kid table in the cafeteria). Maybe they're wealthy in knowledge, skills, and business acumen (maybe they can advise you for free or actively mentor you to greatness).

Interacting with a rich person isn't really anxiety-inducing unless you are hoping they can use their wealth or connection to help you in some way—then suddenly your palms are sweaty, your vision goes wonky, and you're really, really terrified of screwing it up.

But how do you actually talk to these people effectively and without all the hand-wringing?

The 1972 song "Everybody Plays the Fool" by The Main Ingredient offers a useful reminder that sometimes you'll be the one who is loved, and sometimes you'll be the lover. You won't always be the fool, but sometimes you will. You won't always be the adored one, but sometimes you will.

You can apply that same logic to connecting with rich people. In order to be able to receive, you must be able to give. If nothing is flowing in that channel (from rich person to you), you need to create movement in the channel by being a rich person giving to someone in need.

Another way to put it: When I was in my single digits, maybe six or seven, I discovered the wonders of MAIL. Mail was magical—something sent to my house, addressed to ME. But once after getting some birthday cards, my mail dried up and I complained to my mother, who told me an important truth: "If you want to receive mail, you have to send mail." Well, that seemed like a lot of work, but it sure was clarifying, and it was a relief to know there was something I could do. I got a pen pal and began sending and receiving lots of mail.

Let's say you're talking to a "rich person" and you want them to give you a job. First, you need to know what it's like to be in their shoes. If you have never hired someone, hire someone TODAY. Even if it's a ten-dollar job to deliver something or clean out your closet or run a day of errands, make a hire. Post an ad on Craigslist or announce it to the neighborhood kids, field the responses, see what works and doesn't work for you. When you go to ask for your own job, you'll have taken the anxiety out of the process because you'll know what it feels like to be on the other side of the table, doing the hiring and firing. You will know how it feels to be the "rich person," to have something to give, and you'll be able to ask them more persuasively for what you want.

When I was co-editor-in-chief of my college paper, my co-editor, Sarah, and I conducted interviews to see who would replace us. There was one woman I thought would be great for the job, and in the interview, I was pretty tough on her and asked her a lot of questions while my co-editor played "good cop" the whole time. After the meeting, my co-editor was lukewarm about her, but I was going to bat for her. And it occurred to me WOW—had I been on the other side of the table (where I normally am), I would have walked out of that meeting assuming that Sarah really liked me and Krista hated me, even though I wanted her for the job! And now when I take meetings, I'm very aware of how perceptions can be wildly deceiving. This allows me to calm down when people are hard on me, because I know that it's impossible to know what someone thinks of you in those kinds of situations.

Just as you need to know how to be a boss in order to get the job you want, you can learn how to be mentored when you mentor another. I became a much better mentee when I became a mentor. Prior to becoming a mentor myself, I was afraid my mentor would get annoyed if I took up her time, but I discovered that I really *wanted* my mentee to reach out to me more, and that made me feel more confident reaching out to my own mentor.

Here's a practical example from my work life: Once I was casting a short film and it was a mess. We auditioned about thirty actors, but ultimately, the short film fell apart. We didn't get a single day of filming so we didn't follow up with any of the actors. My friend's girlfriend Holiday is an actress and she had a front-row seat to the behind-the-scenes chaos. She was gratified (and maybe a bit surprised) to note that even when she had a good audition, her not being chosen could have nothing to do with her performance; the film might not even end up being made! Seeing the tragedy of our short-lived short film really cheered her up, so I'm glad something good came out of it. If you're an actress auditioning for roles, I recommend you shoot a quick web video and cast some actors, and maybe even pay them twenty dollars. Afterward, you'll probably feel better and thus perform better when it's your turn to audition.

If you want to sell art to clients, go buy some artwork from an artist, even if it's a caricature on the street for a few bucks.

Creating jobs, taking on a mentee, supporting artists—these are all intrinsically good things to do, but they are also extremely effective in learning how to be an employee or a mentee or an artist selling work.

The best leaders are the best followers and vice versa. The best party guests have been party hosts themselves.

And when you participate in this exercise of being on the other side of the table, scale doesn't really matter; it's more the direction of the action that counts. For example, if you are looking for a job and decide you need to experience being an employer, you don't need to provide a salaried sixty-thousand-dollar-a-year position; you can offer a kid five dollars a day to walk your dog. The experience still gives you information and confidence.

So bottom line, if you want mail, send mail.

31. Lush, Feminine Wealth

# CHAPTER 31
# Lush, Feminine Wealth

Adapting an "abundance mind-set" helped get the Pussyhat Project off the ground. I used to think money had to come in a certain "valid" way: for example, make money each day, save up, have a budget, etc. But I discovered that there is another way that is just as valid, and maybe even more accurate, which I think of as lush, feminine wealth. My income comes in chunks—I live the freelance lifestyle, and there's nothing steady about it. A chunk here or a chunk there. I also receive abundance in a lot of different ways—places to stay, artistic patronage, etc. It looks different from the "traditional" way of earning money, I know, but this difference isn't a problem, it's an asset. When I started embracing the different kinds of wealth that come to me—some that comes in W9s and money, some that comes in other forms like inspiration, kind words, support—I feel, and I am, rich.

What I love about lush, feminine wealth is that it is a much more conducive way of looking at the world that supports the creative process. Lush, feminine wealth is also very relatable when you think about nature. Nature doesn't look at her watch and say, "Hmm, it's 9:00 a.m. on a Tuesday, I think I'll grow *this* much in this square of the forest and then I'll take a break." Wealth doesn't function like a manmade machine. It flows like a natural river. The Pussyhat Project GREW in this lush, natural, HUGE way that we're often told is not possible or not realistic, but this is a real phenomenon. And even just ENTERTAINING the thought that however your projects grow, each unique process represents a real, valid way of growth will help your projects do just that—GROW ABUNDANTLY.

When you're gardening, you don't have to grab a vine and tug the tendrils millimeter by millimeter to grow. Lush, feminine wealth is similar. There will be times where there is no visible growth, and then, suddenly, periods of lush growth. And accepting that this is a valid natural part of my life, rather than resisting it and wanting it to look more "responsible" (i.e., mechanized, measurable, and predictable), allows me to free up SO much of my energy to actually create and generate more wealth.

32. Myth of the Crazy Woman

# CHAPTER 32
# Myth of the Crazy Woman

A few months before the Pussyhat Project began, I was on the highly lauded new train connecting Santa Monica and downtown LA for the first time in decades. The city was celebrating with a big free opening weekend. Facebook Live was pretty new then, and quite a few of my guy friends were live-streaming their train trips.

Around 11:00 p.m. I was with a friend on the train, but he was getting off on the first stop while I was getting off on the last stop. After he left, I was harassed by two different men. The first man masturbated at me once the cars got less crowded. The second man followed me out of the subway and blocked my exits, never touching me, but taunting me as he trailed behind, saying he was going to take me to a motel, etc.

I ended up grabbing a Lyft the rest of the way home. I literally had to jump in and close the door on the second harasser.

When I got home, I was so overwhelmed with emotion—anger, sadness, rage. I made a donation to Hillary Clinton that night, my first of many. How is it fair that in this modern world, a man can pay two dollars to get home safely while a woman must pay twenty dollars? Not to mention the emotional stress of being harassed and feeling as though you don't have safe passage through the world.

While the night itself was awful, the following week, when I reported the incident, was an opportunity to see the Myth of the Crazy Woman and how it was holding me back.

Prior to this subway harassment, I had never understood why rape victims didn't report the sexual assault. I remember one night over drinks telling my friend, "If I was raped, I'd tell *everybody*."

I get it now. It was scary to report. I was afraid that I would be accused of lying. I was afraid maybe I didn't see what I saw when the man masturbated. I was afraid that I was making too big of a deal out of the behaviors of two men who didn't actually touch me. I was afraid people would think I was a liar, overly dramatic, or overall *crazy*.

My friend told me that when you see a man masturbating in public, it is such a shock that your brain experiences cognitive dissonance. *That can't be happening*, you think. And that cognitive dissonance sometimes becomes doubt later. *Did I see what I thought I saw? Am I just making this up?*

I was afraid that if cameras didn't back up my story, the sheriff's department would label me a liar and crazy woman *forever*, and whatever I said in the future would not be believed.

Being labeled crazy is scary. My fear of being labeled crazy ought to be completely irrational, but it's not—if so many women are experiencing this same thing, there is something wrong with the world.

After this experience, phrases like "I trust her" and "we believe you" became so important to me. Misogyny is not just hatred of women; it is distrust of women.

This whole book is about speaking up. And when you speak up to those in power, telling them they're wrong, their response is often, "Oh, what you're saying has no value, because you're *crazy*." You can swap out "crazy" with any of these invalidations: lazy, overly sensitive, ungrateful, greedy, attention-seeking, dramatic, whiny, entitled . . .

To erase the Myth of the Crazy Woman we must be aware of the myth and trust our sisters and trust ourselves. If we cultivate this awareness, when the myth is thrown in our faces, we know to call it what it is and not let it stop us from reporting injustices and creating change for the better.

## EXERCISE
### I Believe You

Write this message to five women you think need to hear it: I believe you. I trust you.

You can text them right now. You can add to the message, or simply keep it to "I believe you. I trust you." Even if they are not currently going through an obvious ordeal, they might appreciate hearing this.

You can take a picture of this card on your phone and send it to five people.

33. Scary vs. Dangerous

# CHAPTER 33
# Scary vs. Dangerous

A few years ago, I was a mentor at a ropes course for a group of inner city kids. It was just a week, but it was enough to make an impression. If you don't know, a ropes course is made up of a series of tightropes and rope bridges and climbing nets, all hanging forty feet in the air. You complete the course by strapping on a harness and working through the ropes, all very high up. You climb, you balance, you swing.

I love heights, so this job was great for me, but a lot of the students were understandably frightened. The instructor approached their fear in what I felt was a unique and memorable way. He gathered everyone in a big circle and said, "What you're about to do is scary, but it isn't dangerous." He reminded them that the harnesses were solid, and that he'd double-checked the ropes that morning. Nothing was about to happen to these kids, apart from maybe some rope burns and a comical moment of dangling if someone missed their footing.

The instructor's perspective on fear blew me away. At the time, I'd been working on a book project, and I was terrified of releasing it and hearing people's comments. But thinking through the instructor's advice given to these kids about working high up in this ropes course made me realize that releasing the book might well be scary, but it wasn't dangerous. It wasn't going to kill me.

When it comes to speaking up with respect to issues I'm passionate about, I'm reasonably confident that a lot of us have the same fears: that we'll mess it up somehow or that people won't like us anymore because of it. These voices, or "squelchers," love to whisper that we just shouldn't say what we think, that it would be better and safer if we said nothing. And I get it. Speaking up is scary. But for most of us, it isn't dangerous. However, there are women for whom speaking up *is* dangerous. Women all over the world experience life-threatening violence and death when they speak up. Malala Yousafzai, the youngest recipient of the Nobel Peace Prize, almost died in 2012 when she was attacked by a gunman on her way home from school, and shot through her head, neck, and shoulder. This is in a culture where many people felt girls should not be educated, so by attending school, Malala was labeled a dangerous, outspoken enemy. She was fifteen at the time.

Women in this "danger camp" are women who speak up and thus are in danger of being killed. This is not just a problem in third world countries. In the United States, domestic violence is a leading cause of death for women under fifty. For women who are still alive and in abusive relationships, one can imagine that speaking up might lead to further violence from the abuser (often a man) and death.

In order to change the world, those of us in the "scary camp" (who think of speaking up as scary but who aren't actually in danger) have a duty to use our voices for the sake of those other women, those who know speaking up is a dangerous, subversive risk. The more we do this, the more fears we overcome, the better the world will become. Every time one of us speaks up, both camps are helped.

When we first started this project, I thought to myself, *Wouldn't it be cool if we got women in red states making hats for us? Subversive knitting, right under the noses of their misogynistic neighbors.* And we did that. We did get hats from red states. But there was one hat that sobered my thinking.

We received one hat that had no return address on it. It came with a note. "I'm sorry, I'm not putting my name on this hat. I made this hat for the Women's March in secret, and I had to bring it to the post office in secret. I'm afraid that my husband will find out."

It's not just women in far-flung areas that we have to stand up for. There are women in our own homeland who need us to raise our voices.

34. It's Okay to People Please
(As Long as You're Choosing
Whom You're Pleasing)

# CHAPTER 34

# It's Okay to People Please (As Long as You're Choosing Whom You're Pleasing)

*I used to be so afraid of speaking up. I was like a ghost* on Facebook, reading other people's posts, pressing "like," but never sharing anything about myself. As the 2016 presidential election campaign heated up, I really appreciated reading posts by my friends and colleagues who wrote well-thought-out opinions about the issues on their Facebook pages. The posts really inspired me and helped me feel better about the opinions I was sorting through in my own brain. But I didn't speak up myself.

And then the election happened. Hillary Clinton lost and I examined my fears in a whole new light.

I realized that whether I spoke up or not I was helping *someone*.

If I stayed silent, many people out there would benefit. If I spoke up, many other people out there would benefit. People would benefit no matter what I did, so the question was, who did I want to serve? The answer, obviously, was the people who would benefit from me being LOUD.

Consider that for yourself—that when you are silent about your opinions, there are people like the Koch brothers, and domestic violence abusers, and just the average patriarchal dudes, who benefit. When you are loud, those same people will bristle, but that doesn't matter, because you are helping a whole 'nother group: women, domestic violence victims, young girls who need role models of women who are unafraid to speak up and take up space.

When put that way, it's easy to decide what to do. Speak up.

I think women are much maligned as "people pleasers," but while people pleasing can be detrimental to our progress, it's not detrimental if we are *choosing* the people we please. *Choose* to please the young girls who need role models. *Choose* to serve women who seek equality and liberation. Don't choose to please the patriarchy because you fear reprisal.

Another aspect to consider: When you speak up, not only are you helping a worthy group of people, you are also expressing yourself—and the more you do that, the more you'll see an inherent joy in not hiding your truth. Speaking up is *fun*.

Likewise, making someone a delicious nutritious meal, knitting someone a beautiful gift—all these are people pleasing activities. But not in an obsequious way, no! There is no need to be ashamed of your people-pleasing qualities so long you remember you *choose* whom you want to please, and you stand by your decision of whom you're pleasing (and that you feel empowered to make course corrections as you go!).

I wish I had known this about beauty rituals—as a teenager and well into my twenties, I agonized whether it was "right" to apply makeup or wax my legs. Was I just giving in to patriarchal norms and thus being a bad feminist? What beauty treatments were "okay" to get and what beauty treatments were "too much" and "too vain?" Now I know more about what I like and what I want. I might choose to wax my legs because it pleases me, or pleases my lover, and that is my choice. In that case, waxing my legs is a great decision. But beauty treatments can go astray if they are done out of fear, out of a sense of "no choice." Like, "If I don't wax my legs, everyone in gym class will laugh at me" or "No guy will ever sleep with me" or "I'll get snickers from my female colleagues at work." Don't bother pleasing those people, and don't try to please them when you are in a fearful state. While there's no perfect way to do it, I urge you to try to make decisions from an empowered place. Being sexy is great, but it's not fun being sexy out of fear people will abandon you if you stop. Being sexy is amazing when you know exactly who you're being sexy for, and it's even better if the name on the top of that list is yours.

A reporter recently asked me, "Why is it important for you to make things on your website pretty?"

I stopped in my tracks, because a fear flashed through my mind. "Oh my God, am I just trying to be pretty and pleasing and accommodating? Am I weak? Did I just give in to the patriarchy's need for women to be attractive?"

And the answer is, no. I realized that I wasn't making things pretty for the online trolls who criticized my every decision, and I wasn't making things pretty so patriarchal oppressors would *like* me. I was making things pretty for my people! For my friends. For my followers. For young girls interested in learning more about feminism and speaking up, I wanted kristasuh.com to be an appealing, bright, and happy place for them to visit. It was like making my home appealing for my honored guests. I realized I need not feel any shame for making the site "pretty" and pleasing my visitors because I was actively choosing whom I was serving, and it definitely wasn't the patriarchy.

# CHAPTER 35
# I Stand By It

I once met a guy at a local black box theater, and when it came time to exchange information, I didn't have my card on me, so he gave me his. I was so annoyed, and told him so, because I looooove my business cards. They're letterpressed with painted edges—I love my stationery!

When I got home, I texted him a photo of my business card.

He got back to me right away.

> **Him:** Awesome. Let's gather the troops for a dinner soon.
> :-) )

Hmm . . . a group of my friends had met a group of his friends, so he was referring to the five of us getting together. Maybe he didn't want a romantic one-on-one with me after all.

> **Me:** Yes! You and I === one mind. Great meeting you
> tonight.

**Him:** Same. Speak soon witty bantress . . .

Ahhhhh . . . okay, does that mean something or not?

I very nearly wrote back a complaint that I was always being complimented on my mind but never my sexy body (a joke), but I reeled it back and simply texted him back with

**Me:** Thank you! You're very astute.

This is an actual text exchange with a guy, and every time I looked back at our exchange, I cringed. I was convinced it hadn't conveyed what a witty and suave person I was.

A couple days later (because obviously I was brooding about this two days later), I realized that I could either try to disown these texts that I wrote and groan and berate myself, or I could *stand by it*.

I use this trick now for all my text exchanges. If I text a guy an

awesome flirty joke (better than the ones you see here, I promise!) and he doesn't get back to me right away, instead of anxiously wondering if my joke was offensive or annoying or whatever, I look at my text and say out loud, proudly, "I stand by it."

The act of saying something so serious and monumental as "I stand by it" after texting a pun or a joke is really fun. It always makes me giggle. It also becomes a great beginner introduction to standing by and feeling good about EVERYTHING you do. That is true integrity.

Eventually, when more and more of your work feels as though it stems from your integrity, if someone were to criticize you for it, you could say, "I stand by it," and it would be true.

That feeling of absolute trust in yourself is mind-blowing and earth-shattering. It's living life a different way. What if you could move through the world and know that everything was going to be okay? You will still make mistakes, but no matter what changes, you have the bedrock of knowing that you stand by your actions, knowing what you knew then. It's true confidence.

And it can start so small.

---

EXERCISE

## I Stand By It

Every time you send a text, no matter how inane or mundane, even if it's just "XOXO" or a string of emojis, say, out loud and proudly, "I stand by it."

Have fun with that and then start seeing where else in your life you can start repeating that phrase, and how differently you feel when you do. Perhaps with every purchase you make, you can say, out loud, "I stand by it."

Then, with every piece of artwork or writing or opinion you put out there, say, "I stand by it."

---

36. Valuing Fun

# CHAPTER 36
## Valuing Fun

*I know what you're thinking. You read the title of this* chapter and said to yourself, *Valuing fun? Don't . . . don't we already do that? Because it's . . . fun?* Yes, of course, fun *is* the thing that we look forward to every day, it *is* what we love to display on Instagram, and it *is* the thing that motivates us to make it through the boring parts of our lives. But please, let me invite you to consider where you rank it on your internal list of important-to-do stuff. Is it more or less important than showing up to work on time? Is it more or less important than being there for a friend who's going through a rough patch? Is it more or less important than getting your homework done?

When someone misses an important meeting for a death in the family, we all accept the absence as valid. But if they missed that same meeting because they won the *Hamilton* lottery and snapped two hundred selfies of themselves before and after seeing the show, we'd probably be irritated, possibly even filled with righteous indignation. How dare they have fun when we're all here doing the important stuff? Part of this reaction is jealousy, obviously, but another part of it is the feeling that we're being disrespected. This other person is valuing their own time more highly than mine, but surely *my* time is more important, or at the very least, just as important? The warped thing about this perspective is that because we know how people react when tragedy strikes—usually with kindness and support—as opposed to how people react when something fun happens—with skepticism and accusations of laziness—when we need a break, we may have subconsciously trained ourselves to want that break to come in the form of tragedy. At least then, people won't be snotty about it.

The fact is that we say we know that fun is important, but when it comes to getting through our to-do lists, almost everything else ends up being *more* important than letting loose and having fun. And to some extent, the ability to put off fun—to delay personal gratification—is a crucial and necessary component of overall responsibility. Responsible adults have to get through their work. They have to pay their bills. They have to be able to support other people. Fun isn't a part of those requirements. It's not like a shortage of fun will get them arrested by the Fun Police.

But a life without room for fun is one fenced in by the bare minimum. Working, paying your bills, taking care of your family—these things are the minimum of what we require from people. Personally, I feel like the bare minimum isn't enough. According to a study, by the end of 2016, 55 percent of the American workforce had unused vacation days that neither rolled over into the next year nor could be cashed out. We are literally forfeiting our days off. We are letting them rot, purely because our values have shoved fun and relaxation so far down on the nonexistent importance scale that we've forgotten why we need vacations, relaxation, and moments to unwind. To think we don't need these things is incorrect. The longer we go without a break, the more our work suffers. Our ability to pay attention declines. Our judgment gets spotty. I'm not the only one who has spent time in a work-hole, letting everything else in my life gradually fall apart. Why do we do this to ourselves?

We attach more societal significance to the negative parts of our lives (death, illness, being tired and overworked) than to the things that we should be celebrating (birthdays, vacation, self-care). All parts of life are valid and

EXERCISE

# I Choose vs. I Have to: Accepting Fun in Our Language

If you won *Hamilton* tickets and chose to take the day off of work, would you be tempted to lie and make it sound like you were skipping work because you were sick or had to attend a distant relative's funeral?

If I'm taking a bath and my mom calls me and asks me where I am, I might lie and say I just got out of the shower, because taking a bath sounds too indulgent and fun, while a shower is reasonable and efficient. I'm trying to stop this habit.

If you pay attention, you might find that you are quietly hiding the fun in your life with little language choices.

I realized one day that if someone asked me what I was doing that night, I'd say, "I have to see a friend." And it was like whoa. Hold up. I "have to" see a friend? Seeing a friend is *fun*, so why am I saying I "have to" like it's some chore?

What's kind of crazy is that I say it because it protects me from being judged. I am afraid to say I am choosing to see my friend and have some fun, so instead, I couch it as, "Oh I have to see a friend because I made some prior commitment and you know, I have to be responsible and a good friend and a good citizen."

But in trying to protect myself from being judged, I often will lose sight of my own agency.

Like, let's say it's not a fun thing like seeing a friend, but something that's boring or a hassle.

You don't *have* to do this script, you *choose* to do it, but we tend to lose sight of that. Instead we give over our power to an unspoken patriarchal puritanical work ethic rule. "I have to write this script for work, it's due tomorrow" has all these built-in systems and ideas: deadlines are important, I must be a good worker, only good workers deserve to live.

For both these scenarios, it's infinitely more powerful to say:

For both scenarios, you are not obligated to do anything, and you are the master of your own schedule and your own time, and time is everything.

I was telling my friend Annie that I was working on replacing all the "have tos" in my life with "choose tos." She loved the idea. "I have to try that!" she exclaimed. And then her eyes widened and she turned to face me. "No," she said seriously. "No, *wait*. I *choose* to try that."

---

sacred, and we shouldn't begrudge our neighbors the experiences or objects or moments that make them happy. We need to start truly internalizing the value of pursuing happiness—not just money, not just achievement, but the freedom to go for a walk in the park on a sunny day and watch the squirrels chase each other. We need to celebrate the power of building in moments of elastic, unstructured time in our days, so that we can go back to our work, our passions, and our relationships with a renewed sense of optimism and motivation. We need time, essentially, to simply absorb experience without an agenda.

The Pussyhat Project got a lot of flak for being fun. Shortly before the march the *Washington Post* self-righteously trumpeted, "The Women's March needs passion and purpose, not pink pussycat hats." These naysayers believed the Pussyhat Project "just" involved crafting and silly hats (perhaps this was seen as women's work, and was undervalued for that reason), and we ran into a lot of people who didn't take us seriously. People assumed that because the Pussyhat Project was fun, and literally millions of people were having FUN doing it, including the organizers and architects, that it wasn't a real form of protest. It wasn't strident or earnest or serious enough, although in the end, a photo of a single Pussyhat appeared on the cover of *Time*.

Making the Pussyhat Project fun was the element that made it appeal to people; it made it accessible, enjoyable, and something you could do on your own, in a group, with your family, with your kids, with your grandma. This was the primary reason that the movement spread as far and as fast and as powerfully as it did.

As women, we are told by critics that pain and authenticity will give our cause greater gravitas and respect. When lost in this haze, we forget that fun is *effective*. But fun is *valuable*. Perhaps it is our most undervalued resource when it comes to creating social change. It isn't fluff, it isn't silly, and it isn't a waste of time. We need fun not just in a "break from the rat race" kind of way, but for its intrinsic, unassailable value. Don't be the kind of person who only takes time off for funerals. Be brave enough to make time for fun.

37. Make Plans, Let Them Go

# CHAPTER 37

# Make Plans, Let Them Go

Let me tell you a story. One sunny day, a farmer rescued the baron's daughter from drowning, and the baron was so grateful that he had one of his grooms bring out a handsome roan mare, sturdy and noble. The baron passed the horse's reins into the hands of the farmer and wished him the best of luck. When the farmer brought the horse back to his farm, his neighbors crowded around. "What good fortune!" they said.

The next day, the farmer's son was out riding the new horse when a bird flew out of a thicket. The mare startled and threw the young man from her back. He landed awkwardly, against an outcropping of limestone, and broke his leg. When he limped home, the neighbors crowded around again. "What terrible fortune!" they said.

The next day, as the farmer was out tending his fields, a recruiter from the army approached him. "You have a son, I believe," said the recruiter, flourishing a record book. "Our nation needs young men to go to war." The farmer led the recruiter back to his home, and showed him that his son lay in bed with a broken leg. The recruiter shook his head and went away. He had no place for a boy who wouldn't be able to fight. As he left, the neighbors gathered once more. "What amazing fortune you have," they said to the farmer.

It's hard to value *all* of the things that happen to us, especially when they feel like a stroke of bad luck. Each time something feels like bad luck, there's always a chance that it could turn into a blessing, a stroke of *good* luck—and vice versa. Our triumphs may lead to our downfalls and our tragedies can be the building blocks for our greatest achievements. There's no way to fully take stock of our lives as we're living them, so with that in mind, why try to categorize anything as good or bad luck? Why not just trust that your life will take its course, whatever that may be?

I'm not saying that we have no free will OR that any plans we make are forever doomed. I have a trick for balancing planning and going with the flow, which is simply "Make plans, let them go."

For the Pussyhat Project, we planned and planned and planned, and we ended up having to let go of a lot of it. There's only so much a few people can do to affect the path of a nationwide phenomenon. After a certain point, the Pussyhat Project was fueled by thousands of people across the country making hats and sharing information; it was a movement impossible to micromanage.

You're not going to be able to plan everything out, even if you lose hours and hours of sleep worrying and plotting. I'm not saying planning is useless—far from it: extensive planning is by far the best way for you to invest in your own projects. Dwight D. Eisenhower once wrote, "In preparing for battle, I have always found that plans are useless, but planning is indispensable." Planning makes you think about the ways things might go wrong. It makes you nail down your priorities. It makes your brain flexible enough to take the unknown into account. The more planning you do, the better you can respond when things go off the rails, because this will inevitably happen. But don't make the mistake of assuming that planning can actually prevent the universe from reasserting its dominance.

The flip side of having a plan is giving in to the inevitable chaos that is part and parcel of the workings of the universe. Things will go differently from what you planned; embrace it. It means the universe is cocreating with you. Letting go of plans is less about giving up and more about allowing a higher being to collaborate with you—and often, the universe has ideas grander than you would have ever imagined.

When the unexpected happens, if you've planned enough, you already know what aspects of your project are the most important, and for the rest of it, you can just go with the flow. This combination of planning and going with the flow results in magic. It's certainly better than trying to work against the universe. If the universe has a plan of its own, the more we go with the flow, the more we let the universe work with us, and the more magic we find. And as an additional perk, we experience more happiness in the journey itself.

FREEDOM!

1. 2. 3.

38. Pick Your (3) Battles

# CHAPTER 38
# Pick Your (3) Battles

When I embark on a project—often a script collaboration—I like to choose three things about the project that are very important to me. I'll ask collaborators to do the same. But I definitely do it for myself, because this helps me know how to pick my battles. If something comes up that is not on my list of three things, I'm inclined to let it go, or I'll discuss it and have an opinion but not fight to the death about it. But if it's one of my three deal breakers that people want to change, it's an absolute no, and I take my project elsewhere. It makes decision-making so much easier and cleaner.

For example, I worked on a script set in a Chinese restaurant. My three things: I wanted an Asian-American cast, including the star; I wanted the star character to be a late bloomer; and I wanted it to be a smart comedy. I brought on a collaborator and when the show *Fresh Off the Boat* came out, my collaborator asked what I thought about changing the setting of our show to a nail salon, because *Fresh Off the Bo*at had a Chinese-American family restaurant and this seemed similar to ours. I think he was surprised when I said "sure" so easily—and I explained to him it was because the family's business itself wasn't one of my three things. There was also a grandma character that was sometimes in, sometimes out, depending on the draft, and I was fine with that, because she wasn't one of the deal-breaking three.

For the Pussyhat Project, I wanted the people knitting—our collaborators—to have *freedom*. I didn't want to dictate every stitch they made. For that project my three things were: hats must be pink (any shade) and hats must be handmade (knitted, crocheted, sewn, whatever!). There wasn't even a third thing. We preferred cat ears, and they eventually became iconic to the pussyhat, but we didn't want to exclude anyone or give people too many directions either. Young children could make hats without ears on loom kits and they were so happy. The variety and creativity this freedom inspired was amazing to see. People made balaclava pussyhats, pride pussyhats, literal vagina pussyhats, and it was SO cool.

---

**EXERCISE**

## My Three Things

Think of a project you're working on and come up with the three things that are most important to you about it (i.e., if any of these three things are not met, it would no longer feel like your project). The project could be a book, a revolution, a vacation, a relationship, a living situation, an apartment, a new job, setting up a yoga studio, or securing a birthday party venue.

---

39. Schmoozing

# CHAPTER 39
# Schmoozing

*In order to be an ace networker, you need to play the fool.*

I used to enter social situations thinking that I needed to be ALL KNOWING and SUPER SMART in order to successfully handle any interaction. I thought I could only be a successful networker if I controlled everything. I obsessed about what other people were "really" thinking about me.

This (of course) meant that I felt paranoid and self-conscious about what people said or did and what that could possibly MEAN about me; usually, in my fear-driven mind, most of the time whatever they did, whatever action they took, meant that they didn't like me.

This is where playing the fool totally helps.

If you are thinking a person dislikes you, but you are playing the fool, you pretend everything is fine, unless it becomes necessary to address it (which rarely, rarely happens and thus saves you a lot of time and energy from worrying. Remember: the worry dance in chapter 20 is always optional).

Example: Let's say there's a potluck and I come to the party with my chicken and capers dish. (This is a lie, since I don't cook, but we'll pretend.)

As I set my dish down on the table, I overhear a woman in a gorgeous dress sniff and say loudly, "I *hate* capers."

The drama-loving, fear-induced ego voice in me is *on that* lightning quick. The voice offers these awful scenarios that it probably finds "helpful": "Oh my God, she hates you, she doesn't want you here, yours is the only dish here with capers in it, so she obviously means you. She probably dislikes you because she's jealous—not of your dress, because clearly hers is better, but maybe because last time you were at Sam and Molly's . . . "

This voice is kind of like a paranoid private detective I don't remember hiring and now I'm stuck with him and his "helpful" observations. I used to let that voice run away and drag me down with it. Now I simply say, in my head, "Thank you. Noted." And I picture putting these "helpful" observations in a file folder and never looking in that file folder unless the woman in front of me does something outright antagonistic or harmful. I'll already have a file to consult, but in the meantime, I don't have to worry.

I also then invite the fool voice to speak up.

If I were to play the fool, and I heard, "Oh my God, I hate capers," the only thing the fool has to say is, "Maybe she just really dislikes capers. This has nothing to do with me."

It's helpful to note that this is a far less scandalous, far less "fun" story, because, well, there is no story. It's almost boring. Compare the drama of "she hates you" to "she doesn't like capers." Yes, it's boring, but the "boring" story can lead to far more peace of mind and allow you to focus on exciting projects that are expanding your life, not drama-filled scenarios that are constricting it.

Playing the fool helps a lot in reducing conflict too. For example, if someone were to say to you, "Who do you think you are?" most of us would be offended. The fool is happier, though, and simply takes the question for what it is, at its face value. *Hmm, who do I think I am? I'm Krista, I'm a writer.*

When you play the fool, you never have to give in to other people's conflict, freeing up space for yourself to have fun with creative endeavors.

EXERCISE

# Social Anxiety Annihilators

Say this affirmation ten times and write it down a hundred times in your journal. Repeat as often as necessary.

 *When people see me, they smile.*

 *When I speak, people are eager to hear what I have to say.*

 *When I leave, people think of me fondly.*

## Bonus:

You can customize the affirmation for yourself even more by pinpointing exactly what part of a social interaction scares you, and then coming up with an affirmation for that.

That's how I made this affirmation—I was afraid when people saw me, they'd roll their eyes, so instead I affirm that when they see me, they smile. I was afraid that when I spoke, people would tune me out, so I affirmed that they'd lean in, eager to hear what I have to say. I was afraid that when I left, people would snicker about me, and instead I imagined them thinking of me fondly.

This affirmation worked wonders for me. When I would go out to network, if I felt my old fears arise, like, "Oh, now that I've left, they are rolling their eyes and snickering at me," the affirmation training I had done reminded me that it was possible that they could be thinking of me fondly. It would soothe my fears until the fears mostly disappeared whenever I went out to network.

A few months after I started this exercise, a friend told me out of the blue, "Krista, whenever you open your mouth to speak, I am so eager to hear what you have to say."

## Shame the Verb and Shame the Noun

My life coach was on a boat with some people she had just met, and the people were actively shaming her about her job. "Do you make money doing that?" "How can you charge so much?" Instead of getting upset, she answered their questions calmly. As she told me this, it occurred to me, "Wow, there is the *verb* shame, but no *noun* shame. People are shaming her, and yet, there is no shame in the room because she is not producing any. She stays shame free, and she gives none of her power away."

You can do this too. If someone asks you a question that is shaming, like, "Who do you think you are?" you can simply play the fool and answer back honestly, with no shame at all attached.

## Two-Way Street

Networking is a two-way street, and not every interaction has to be a win. Sometimes you won't connect with someone, and that's okay. Sometimes it's gonna be your "fault" and sometimes it's gonna be their "fault." I put "fault" in quotes because at the end of the day, there's no need to ascribe blame; it simply wasn't a good connection and you're both better off elsewhere. I mention fault, though, because sometimes high-achieving women can self-flagellate and I like to remind them (as well as myself) that the other person in the interaction could have done more too. Maybe it's their fault, and also, maybe it's no one's fault.

40. No Secondary Emotions
and How to Get On
The Joy Spiral

# CHAPTER 40
# No Secondary Emotions and How to Get on the Joy Spiral

*Happy people get shit done! A super-simple way to be* all holy and Zen and peaceful and happier than all your neighbors is to cut out secondary emotions.

What do I mean by "secondary emotions"?

Well, let's say I'm sad. Sadness is my primary emotion. Let's say I'm angry that I am sad. Perhaps I'm angry because I feel I shouldn't be sad over a silly thing. Anger is my secondary emotion.

Imagine I acted out on my secondary emotion with someone—they would get the blast of my anger, but we wouldn't get to the primary emotional matter: my sadness.

Furthermore, let's say there are MORE emotions piled on top of this. Let's say I'm annoyed that I'm angry that I'm sad, because I should know better than to add secondary emotions to my primary emotion. And then let's say I'm fearful that I'm annoyed that I'm angry that I'm sad because I ought to be more loving to myself. This becomes a vicious cycle, a downward negative shame spiral.

So no negative secondary emotions! Because negative secondary emotions can happen to amazing primary emotions. For example, have you ever felt really happy and then felt really guilty for feeling happy?

If you stick to your primary emotion, positive or negative, you will allow yourself to feel your feelings without piling on heavy, useless, secondary emotions and you will more quickly be able to process your feelings and move on.

Now here's one wild joyous exception: *positive secondary emotions.*

This is going to blow your mind.

Imagine if whatever primary emotion you have, you highly approve of it and tack on a positive secondary emotion. And another and another.

I'm feeling content.

I'm happy that I'm content.

I'm elated that I'm happy that I'm content.

I'm proud that I'm elated that I'm happy that I'm content.

See how this can keep going and going?

What you're on now is the opposite of the shame spiral; you're on *the joy spiral.*

If you're not feeling so joyful right now, you don't have to try to hop on a joy spiral, especially if it feels difficult and forced. I like to think of it like training a puppy. One trick is that when you need to teach a puppy to sit, instead of pushing his butt down and saying, "Sit. Sit," you go about your day and wait until you see him naturally sitting and then you pounce on him with tons of positive reinforcement. "Sit! You're sitting! Good boy! Good sit. Good sit."

Similarly, you don't have to force yourself to be happy to try the joy spiral exercise; you can simply wait until you do feel a positive glimmer and then build on that with tons of positive secondary emotions. For example, one afternoon you might think, "I feel pretty okay." *Omg, this is it!* the trainer in you will scream! And then you'd try the joy spiral: "I feel happy that I feel pretty okay. I feel proud that I feel happy that I feel pretty okay. I feel ecstatic that I feel proud that I feel . . . "

And so on.

A really advanced move is to create a joy spiral from a negative emotion. Human beings are on this earth to experience the entirety of life. So you're going to feel a whole range of emotions including the "negative" ones. But you can be happy about that.

> I feel angry.
>
> I feel proud that I feel angry because in the past I haven't been very good at allowing myself to be angry.
>
> I feel happy that I feel proud that I feel angry.

> I feel sad.
>
> I feel happy that I feel sad because that means I'm processing the loss of a loved one.

> I feel numb.
>
> I feel hopeful that I feel numb because that means I might be processing grief differently from everyone else around me and that's okay.

To be the happiest person in your neck of the woods, the one who creates, accomplishes, and works with a smile and a song, try noting when you're tacking on negative secondary emotions and release them to focus on your primary emotion. And when you find an opportunity to go on a joy spiral by adding positive secondary emotions, go for it and take that joyous ride upward!

41. Recalibrate Your Rules:
Do Magic. Whether You
Believe in It or Not

# CHAPTER 41

# Recalibrate Your Rules: Do Magic Whether You Believe in It or Not

There is magic in taking mundane objects and creating divine meaning out of them. The pussyhats were magic—women's rights supporters took ordinary inert pink yarn and created the symbol of a movement charged with meaning.

You don't have to believe in magic, but I encourage you to try it on for size and see if it serves you or helps you become more creative. I encourage everyone, for fun, to see an astrologer or a natal chart reader, or see a tarot card reader, or to do a free online natal chart or tarot card spread.

When we are feeling stuck and when our lives are not going well or the way we'd like them to, it's usually because we are fixated on the same thoughts and haven't recalibrated for a while. Seeing a tarot card reader, even if you don't believe, is a way to open yourself up to new thoughts in a fun way. A masseuse gets to physical areas you haven't worked on in a while, and moves the muscles around in ways you haven't on your own. A tarot card reader does the same thing for your thoughts. Think of a tarot card reader as a writer or performer who's making a performance on the spot just for you, and see what inspiration, if any, you get out of this artistic show.

I had been dating this guy for almost two years. I felt stuck and unhappy, but I was afraid to break up with him because he was a good guy, and while I knew there were plenty of fish in the sea, I was afraid that most of the fish were icky and that the most I could hope for after breaking up with him was a lateral move. If I was just going to find a similar guy who would also have flaws that I would come to dislike, why not stick with the one I've got?

I was buying a gift for a friend in a store in Los Angeles that had tarot card reading booths in the back. I ran into one of the readers and she said something so spot-on I had to go in for a reading. The skeptic in me said that maybe she was Googling me and then using expert showmanship to dupe me, but I didn't care because she helped me. She sensed a guy in my life that was a "major interference" and said that if I broke up with him by the end of December, I would meet a new guy, likely an Aquarius, in March. "He is a King, all the other men around you are Knights." My friends started calling this foretold lover "the Aquarius King." It may sound silly, but the way she worded it, the way she foretold it, was the first time I could even imagine life beyond this current boyfriend.

I broke up with the boyfriend and it was one of the best decisions of my life. I was able to focus on my career without worrying about what he thought. March whizzed by and I realized that I had never met the Aquarius King, but it didn't matter, I was happy.

And also, maybe the reader wasn't wrong—she said the Aquarius King would come if I broke off my relationship by the end of December. I broke it off a few days into January. So . . . she's technically still right!

The key here is that it doesn't matter how help comes to you, if it's helpful, take it for what it is, helpful.

# The Swan that Broke My Rules

There's a darling little gift store near my office that I'll often walk to in order to get inspired and/or procrastinate. One day, in the baby book section, I saw the cutest array of stuffed animals in a bassinet, and of all the bunnies and bears and foxes, I could not take my eyes off this ginormous stuffed swan. It was gorgeous and Elizabeth Taylor–esque in that it had no qualms about taking up space and being beautiful. I wanted it so much. But I didn't buy it. I didn't need it, I wasn't a kid anymore, and when I was quite young, around the age of twelve, I made a rule for myself that I didn't need to buy myself stuffed animals anymore.

A few weeks later I was back. I fell in love with the swan again, decided not to buy it again, and then suddenly was like, "WHY?"

I had a rule about not buying stuff I didn't need, but I have learned to relax that rule. I mean, I bought all this pink yarn I didn't need, but it later inspired me to do the Pussyhat Project, so I learned to trust my instincts when I wanted something. And as for the rule of not buying stuffed animals for myself—well, that was another rule I could change. I asked myself, "Does this rule still serve me?" It did at one time, when I was young and insatiable for toys and would have driven my family out of house and home with my stuffed animal habit. But I could tell that the rule wasn't useful for me now; that I wouldn't go on a binge simply because I bought one stuffed swan. The rule had served me before, and now it no longer did.

I bought that swan.

And it has given me so much joy. I carry it around with me to the office, to sushi, when I'm driving. It's a fun disrupt to people's day. My friends like to coo over it like it's my baby. I'm not saying it's going to be with me forever, but for now, it's like my new accessory or pet. It watches over me when I write. It's playful and "useless" and wonderful.

I think we come up with all these constricting rules and depressing stories about how the world works, and in our heart of hearts, we hope someone is going to come in and prove all of those stories wrong. For example, you might have rules about dating and stories about how dating never works, but secretly wish that someone will come in and defy all expectation and you will fall in love with him and get married. Maybe the swan was like that for me. I had sworn off all stuffed animals and then I met the Stuffed Animal One that I could not resist, and I broke down all my rules for him. So romantic!

The real point here, though, is that your rules are always able to be changed—it's entirely up to you. I recommend you keep to a rule for two to eight weeks to really test it out, but even then, if it's really not serving you, you are free to release a rule anytime you please!

## I Know Better

During most of my twenties I had a mantra running (sometimes subconsciously) through my head: "You know better." This made me an excellent learner, because I was open to all sorts of knowledge from all sorts of sources. I was an excellent mentee, because I trusted my mentor to know better, and I firmly believed in not having to learn things the hard way if I didn't have to—I resolved to learn from other people's mistakes so I didn't have to repeat them. I was a good beauty client too—if I got a haircut I would automatically trust whoever it was styling me. "You're the expert, you know better."

But in my late twenties, right around twenty-nine, I started to see how this rule was ceasing to serve me well. For example, I'd need to make a decision and I'd be going through my list of mentors and experts, gathering information, when really, I could have saved time and just chosen any option and it would have been fine. I found that not all professional aestheticians were good or understood my needs and my body. I discovered, instead, a thought I found somewhat terrifying: "*I* know better."

That's such a scary thing to say, especially in a world that sneers at women who say, "I know better." The sneers say, "No, you don't," or whisper, "You're uppity. Your pride will be your downfall."

But the phrase was also terrifying because it was just so foreign to me. All through my twenties—and my teens and childhood too—I had operated according to the belief that "you know better," and it had really served me. It was scary at first to start saying, "I know better, I know what is right for me," but it was ultimately rewarding.

As I said in the very first chapter, everything changes, and I'm now at a time where "I know better" is serving me well. Someday the thought "You know better," may serve me again. The pendulum will swing back and forth (sometimes several times in a day), and the less resistance we have to changing our guiding thoughts as needed, the healthier and more effective we become.

**EXERCISE**

## Thirty Outlandish Wishes

Write a list of thirty outlandish wishes. Make them big, make them irrational, make them bend the rules of space and time. Get detailed, get lost in each fantasy. This exercise will help you shed the upper limit of what you think is possible.

Revisit this list in a few months and see if any of them have come true (perhaps in spirit if not in letter!).

42. Try New Things

## CHAPTER 42

# Try New Things . . . to Find Your Superpower and Increase Your Creativity

*"Because it builds character." This is a thing parents* say, right? Do your homework because it builds character. Finish your chores because it builds character. Try new things because it builds character.

I disagree. While trying new things builds character, I prefer a more exciting reason: *because you gotta find your secret superpower!*

Admit it, you believe you have a secret superpower, waiting to be discovered. You've never ridden a horse in your life, but the unruliest stallion in the stable that's never been broken is putty in your hands and lets you hop right up on his back. You're not a pole dancer, but somehow you're so naturally gifted at it that you get a standing ovation the first time out.

I mean, yes, this is all somewhat far-fetched, but a girl can dream, right? And the thing is, there are so many things in the world to do, it's inevitable that you're going to be really good at at least one of them on your first try. The trick is to try a bunch of things that interest you, have fun with them, and be happily surprised when you find your superpower.

For example, I took a class at Magnolia Bakery, a well-known bakery in Los Angeles, and literally the very first rose I iced was *perfect*. People *ooh*ed and *ahh*ed. I was elated. I'd found a secret superpower! I also took classes that I was *not* good at, but still enjoyed immensely. I was literally the worst student in contortion class. At a circus school training center, I joined a group of ladies twice a week. For an hour, we would sit in a circle in various positions that the teacher would demonstrate. Then the teacher would go around the circle, kind of like you did as a kid for Duck, Duck, Goose, and she would use her petite frame to PUSH us deeper into the stretch. It was a fun class of chatter punctuated with masochistic screams. Did I mention I was literally the worst? I've never been so obviously the worst in my entire life. The class was fun, and I admit, it was even character building for me. After a lifetime of academic overachieving, it's so useful to experience being the worst at something and finding that I'm still okay, I'm still alive, and I'm still a valid human being.

Trying new things also increases your creativity by a magnitude of about 14.977. Creativity is all about making surprising connections, so it makes sense that if you try new things, you have more opportunities to make interesting and unique connections.

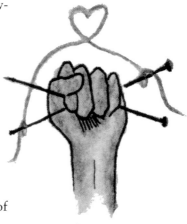

I tried crocheting and knitting a sweater for the first time in the summer of 2016 and got obsessed with it. There was no real justification for doing this. I lived in Los Angeles, where you might need a sweater a few days out of

**EXERCISE**

## Creative Matrix

Write down three skills you have.

A.

B.

C.

Write down three hobbies you have or want to try.

1.

2.

3.

Now write an idea for how the skill and hobby can be combined—no idea is too outlandish!

1A.

1B.

1C.

2A.

2B.

2C.

3A.

3B.

3C.

the year; buying machine-made sweaters is generally cheaper than making it myself; I wasn't making a living as a knitter. But had I not allowed myself to try this new thing, when election day rolled around, and when plans for the Women's March came together, I don't think I would have come up with the Pussyhat Project. If I had been a screenwriter without the recent knitting obsession, trying to come up with a way to contribute to the Women's March, I might have been thinking in old frameworks like, "Write a movie about the march," "Produce a documentary about women," etc. In this case, my experience as a Hollywood writer-producer (writing, organizing, collaborating) joined with my obsession for knitting, and a really cool new project came together, one that started a *movement*.

Obviously, the combinations are endless! What if your skill with woodworking was combined with your love of ice cream and you built waffle structures that look like doll furniture but that *also held ice cream in them*. Okay, maybe that's a stretch, but you can come up with all sorts of ideas!

43. Criticisms, Dismissals, and Panthers in the Dark

# CHAPTER 43
# Criticisms, Dismissals, and Panthers in the Dark

Criticism hurts. That's okay. I used to think if I were truly powerful then criticism would never touch me, but criticism can sting no matter how successful you are. When it comes to criticism from people you don't know in person, I think there are two types of critics—Collaborators Once Removed and the Traumatized.

Think of a TV show that has hugely devoted fans. The kind of show where audiences write fan fiction online, using the characters in their own stories. The kind of show where people live-tweet the episodes and make demands of the head writer to have two characters finally fall in love.

When these fans are critiquing the series, they are people who are passionate and wish they could make the show or collaborate on it. They can't get into the writer's room so they instead write fan fiction and strongly worded letters to the showrunner. They admire what the show is doing or its reach. It's like the series is a gladiator in the ring, and the fans want to be in the arena too. If they critique something you did or made after the fact, imagine if they were alongside you in the creation process—they might have some interesting ideas, and you could take it or leave it. The critics who are Collaborators Once Removed can be helpful; they could even inspire you, though you don't need to feel you must take their suggestions.

The second type of critic is the Traumatized. Sometimes, you might get a criticism that is not collaborative or constructive at all. It might be purely ad hominem, like something along the lines of "How dare you" but with more colorful language. When that happens to me, I think of this quote from the book *The Body Keeps Score* by Bessel Van der Kolk, MD:

> The need for attachment never lessens. Most human beings simply cannot tolerate being disengaged from others for any length of time. People who cannot connect through work, friendships, or family usually find other ways of bonding, as through illnesses, lawsuits, or family feuds. Anything is preferable to that godforsaken sense of irrelevance and alienation.

As odd as it sounds, this type of critic is trying to bond with you. Think about it; if this critic were fully satisfied in other areas of his life, like work, friendships, and family, he wouldn't have the time or need to reach out to you, a stranger, and tell you what he thinks of you. But he fears being irrelevant and alienated, so a strongly worded tweet or email to you is a small salve for him. The sense of self-righteousness and action gives him a moment's reprieve from irrelevance. He'd rather attach, connect, and bond in an unloving way than be totally alienated.

While it's not an immediate cure-all, I find that when I receive criticism, I can remind myself that the critics are Collaborators and/or the Traumatized and it helps me get out of a purely reactive defensive state.

- - - - - - - - - - - - - -

**EXERCISE**

## Panther in the Dark

Use the mantra "I am a panther in the dark." In your journal, write it over and over again until it fills the page.

### Bonus:

Come up with your own mantra, get creative!

My friend Yumi Sakugawa is a comic book writer, and hers is,

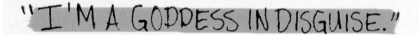

"I'M A GODDESS IN DISGUISE."

My friend Anthony Goulet says,

"YOU ARE A BLESSING, A MIRACLE, AND A GIFT.
SOMEONE'S FAILURE TO SEE YOU AS A BLESSING,
A MIRACLE, AND A GIFT DOES NOT TAKE AWAY THE
FACT THAT YOU ARE A BLESSING, A MIRACLE, AND A GIFT."

- - - - - - - - - - - - - -

Criticism hurts, but so do dismissals. If you ever feel you are dismissed, ignored, or underestimated, I like to use a trick I call "panther in the dark." It's a mantra. I simply say, out loud or in my head: *I am a panther in the dark*. It means that even though I am not acknowledged, it doesn't mean I don't exist. Just because I am not seen doesn't mean I am not still there. I can feel myself as the panther, lying in wait, her muscles powerful and waiting to spring into action the moment I decide it's time.

There will be times when you feel you must speak up, and you might falter. You might let the opportunity pass. Do not fear. While I want all women to speak up more, I don't expect you to speak up perfectly. I don't expect you to speak up every single time. When you miss an opportunity to speak up, you must not be so hard on yourself. Instead, say to yourself, "I am a panther in the dark." You are ready to speak up the moment you deem it is time to pounce.

44. The Cherry on Top

# CHAPTER 44
# The Cherry on Top

Picture this: You have the perfect tall, fluted glass with scalloped edges. It's filled with ice cream—the vanilla has vanilla bean flecks, maybe you've got rich chocolate and creamy strawberry in there too. Then you take a can of whipped cream and with that distinctive vacuum sound, you spiral out a perfect little mountain. Maybe you top it with nuts and pour chocolate syrup on it all, letting it ooze its way down the spirals into the gaps made by the scoops of ice cream, all the way down to the bottom of the glass. Gorgeous, right? But also missing something.

The cherry on top is the perfect finishing touch to all of this awesomeness. You grab a maraschino cherry and gently nestle it at the tip of the mountain. And there it is, a sweet and delicious flag—a bright pop of red—on top of your creation. And when did a perfectly crafted ice cream sundae with a shiny red cherry NOT make a person happy?

Here's my cherry on top wisdom: when you feel overwhelmed, eat a sundae! Yes, do that, but also read on.

There is a Zen koan that simply states, "It's already done. It's never done." No matter what you're working on—your novel, raising your child, a project for work—you can apply either of those statements and find reasons for each to be true. It follows that since either one of these state-ments can be true at any given time, it makes sense to *choose* the one that best serves you in the moment.

When I feel overwhelmed, what helps me is to choose "it's already done." You'll actually hear me muttering to myself, "It's already done" or "This is just the cherry on top."

Here's a specific example of how the cherry-on-top way of looking at the world has helped me. With the Pussyhat Project, after the six-day cru-cible period and after the launch, there was an overwhelming sense of, "It's never done." There were emails that needed replies, reporters to coax into writing a story (this is before they came running after *us*), social media posts to update and improve on. We were constantly engaged in spreading the word and adding allied yarn stores. The "it's never done" statement was freaking me out. It made me harried and panicked. Although some people may respond to that mantra, thinking, "There's always something more to do, so what's the point, anyway? I might as well do what I can," that's great. If that statement works for you, by all means *use it*. But for me, I preferred my chipper ice cream metaphor: "it's already done, this is just the cherry on top." It relaxed me, and made me feel that I could put forth my best effort, and enjoy myself while I was doing so.

We already had the base of the sundae, we had the idea, the manifesto, the website, the reach out, the release. No matter what, *the Pussyhat Project was happening*. Even if the hat collection point in DC failed—if we *roy-ally* screwed up there and, I don't know, say, lost all the packages—there were STILL going to be hats showing up at the march through other means (marchers were bringing pussyhats themselves, for instance). Even if we didn't answer every email or follow up with every potential celebrity, that was okay. The sundae was already there. Anything I did after that was just the cherry on top. Having this attitude made me calm down. I realized that I could relax and do whatever I wanted to do for the project. I didn't need to freak out about whether it would be executed perfectly or whether it would work. We already had our beautiful, well-crafted, and delicious-looking sundae. These two months of additional work were the cherry on top.

I believe that too often women especially treat every new task in their life as the base of the sundae, when really, we have built this sundae MANY times over (you know it's true!), and we could easily see this task as a simple cherry-on-top scenario.

I think there is a fear that if we don't treat every task as if it's the foundational end-all be-all, we will fail. That we *need* this pressure in order to ever accomplish anything in life.

But is that true? What if we could relax into our work a bit, enjoying the feeling of being accomplished, of having goals and tasks. What if we relieved the pressure? Would we fail? No way.

I've applied the cherry-on-top philosophy to my entire life, not just my work, and it's made me happier, more productive, and (most important) less stressed out.

## Life Accomplishments: I'm Already Enough. Everything I Do Is Extra

In August of 2015, I had a revelation that I was creating out of shame, and that was why my projects weren't taking off. Every time I had an idea for something, I put so much pressure on it, because it *had* to succeed. It wasn't about the doing of the project; it was about the outcome. I *needed* it to succeed in order to feel good about myself. As a result, I was overly attached to the outcome, and this stymied my creativity in a very real way. In other words, the mojo was gone. I felt that I had to achieve success in my creative career in order to deserve being here on earth. I had conflated being a good human being with being a successful human being. I was ashamed of being alive without *accomplishing* anything.

That's a lot of pressure to put on an infant idea just coming into the world. Imagine if we approached a baby like that? We never would!

If I let go of that shame, I was afraid that I would lose a desire to create anything again; that without the pressure to accomplish, a pressure fueled by shame, I would just become a lazy slacker loser. How could I create from a new place that wasn't rooted in shame?

The word came to me quietly: "curiosity." And from that moment on, I tried with all my might to make sure I created from curiosity, not shame. As it turns out, kicking shame to the curb was the best thing I ever did for my creativity. Maybe shame is the thing that's stopping you as well.

Instead of barging into an arena intent on *winning*, I let myself be guided into projects based on what I was curious about. By letting go of shame as the primary motivation, I found that I did not become an unproductive couch potato; in fact, I became more productive (because it turns out, shaming yourself takes up a lot of energy—freeing that up gave me more energy to produce!).

But how I got there was a harrowing inner journey: I literally had to sit down and imagine, REALLY imagine, what life would be like if I *never accomplished anything. Ever. Ever. Ever.*

This was terrifying to imagine, because superstitiously I didn't even want to go there in my mind, as if thinking about it might make it come true, or attract some weird slacker energy into my life, creating a vicious cycle. But I knew I had to find out what lay at the end of this little self-imposed exercise. So I sat with it. I imagined myself five years from now, ten years from now, fifty years from now. Each decade whizzing by without any accomplishment whatsoever. Instead, I just *lived*. I kept wanting to look away, but instead I kept my mind's eye on this visualization.

What I found was that if I never accomplished anything in this lifetime . . . I would be okay. I would be just fine. I would still be a good person, a worthwhile person, a person worthy of space on the earth, and worthy of love. I would still give joy to other people, as I did at the time. And making others happy wasn't what *earned* my right to be here on earth; rather, it was a symptom of a deeper condition of just being *inherently okay*, and feeling like I was inherently deserving and worthwhile.

EXERCISE

# Baby Pictures

If you have baby pictures, take them out and look at them. You will feel instant love and affection for this little being caught in Kodachrome. And if you think about it, whatever age you are now, you are *way* more accomplished than that little beast in the photo. I can now walk, I am potty-trained, I can talk, I went to school, I got a degree, I've made people laugh. I'm sure you can come up with your own list. You are so accomplished, and yet you are so hard on yourself. You see this baby photo and feel pure love, even though Baby You is so *unaccomplished*. What does that say? That you are inherently lovable without accomplishments. Achievements don't make you a worthy person, your very existence does.

A note about babies and the Pussyhat Project: I'm half Chinese and half Korean (and all American!) and I think the "tiger mom" phenomenon coined by Amy Chua was really true for me. I was expected to accomplish and achieve at all times. As the Pussyhat Project grew, I began to look at it as if it were my child, but I didn't play the role of tiger mom. I talked to it and I told it, "No matter how big or small you get, I will always love you, I will always be proud of you." Essentially, I was the opposite of a tiger mom, who insinuates that you are worthless unless you get a perfect score. I didn't want to put that type of pressure on my "child," the Pussyhat Project. And it was true, I *did* love it, I *do* love it, no matter what size it is. And I do think because I loved it unconditionally, the project grew to enormous proportions and had tremendous impact. It was beloved by so many people, and when love is poured on a child, he or she can do amazing things, and feel amazing as well.

I've mentioned the cherry on top in terms of projects, but what if you filtered EVERYTHING you do in your life through the cherry on top philosophy? You were born, and that is the sundae. Everything that follows is, literally and metaphorically, the cherry on top. Everything you do is *optional*, extra, bonus, a beautiful add-on touch to the already amazing sundae of your life, of you. It doesn't mean you'll stop doing anything worthwhile, but it might mean you do worthwhile things without feeling like the whole sundae will topple unless you do it right. You might be able to do the same job but better—and in better spirits—if you think of it as the cherry on top.

45. I Am the Bee in
the Swimming Pool

# CHAPTER 45
# I Am the Bee in the Swimming Pool

Once I was swimming in an outdoor community pool in Los Angeles and I noticed a bee that was drowning. Its wings were bogged down with water and it had nothing solid to rest on in order to dry off and launch into flight. I didn't want to touch the bee because I had once gotten stung and didn't want to repeat that painful experience. With no tools nearby, I simply started pushing the water, creating waves to push the bee toward the tiled wall of the pool. It took a lot more time and wave-making than I had anticipated (I couldn't make the waves too big lest the bee be totally pulled under) but it seemed sadistic to do too small of a wave and prolong the process. It was a delicate alchemy of pushing the water and waiting for a wave to carry the bee further to safety.

Every time a strong Krista-made wave pushed the bee toward the wall, I couldn't help but anthropomorphize the bee. If I were the bee, I would be so pissed, so in agony at the moment. *Why, WHY, God, are you doing this to me?* And in this scenario, I suppose I was playing God, and I wished there was some way to communicate to the bee, "I know this sucks, little

bee dude, but honestly, I'm helping you, because this is going to *save* you."
After a few minutes, the bee was near the wall of the pool and I gave it one
last gentle wave and its bee feet met the tile of the pool wall. It stayed there
a moment, and slowly the water evaporated and it was able to come fully
onto the "dry land" of the wall. A few minutes later, it flew away, free, and,
as I had promised, SAVED.

Now, whenever I am in mental or emotional pain but I know overall
that my life is going in a good direction, I remind myself that I am the bee in
the swimming pool, and it's all going to be all right.

---

**EXERCISE**

## Pronoia

Whenever it feels like the whole world is against you, imagine that this
is all an elaborate plan to make your life better. Some call this pronoia:
a great conspiracy looking out for your best interests. Write down a
scenario, no matter how preposterous, in which this is the case (have fun
with it!), and note how you feel afterward. Giving your mind the freedom
to entertain these possibilities can give you a greater sense of agency.

46. Throwing a Party

# CHAPTER 46
# Throwing a Party

*If you can throw a party you can be politically active.*
I'm telling you: throwing a party means you are organized, powerful, and you know how to communicate with people (via words and VISUALS), and you know how to handle logistics, marketing, etc. Don't shy away from being active in politics or organizing politically because you feel like you don't have the skills. If you've ever thrown a party, if you've ever gathered people for a knitting circle or a celebratory dinner, you KNOW how to organize politically.

There are so many worldwide causes that we care about, and party planning can help us address them all. We need to stop gerrymandering, protect *Roe v. Wade*, get out the vote, stop men's violence against women, stop rape culture, raise awareness and stop shame about reaching out to suicide prevention resources, stop homelessness, help reduce student debt . . . It's a lot, right? And that's just the start of one list. No doubt you have many more issues you would add (and should) to your own list of issues you're passionate about.

Like I said, we *can* address them all—through party planning. Here's how:

- — — — — — — — — — — — — — —

**EXERCISE**

## Party for Peace

1. Pick one or two causes you care the most about (this will help you feel less scattered and hopeless, and give you time for self-care).

   Great! You are now a party host for that cause.

2. Organize "cause parties" for those issues in such a way that you allow other people to come as guests.

3. Attend other people's cause parties that you want to support as a party guest, just as they show up for your cause parties.

- — — — — — — — — — — — — — —

Say you're hosting a dinner party: you might accept help from a well-meaning guest who wants to help with the dishes, but if after awhile you're putting *all* your guests to work, they're not really guests anymore. Similarly, when you're a leader for a cause, you design and host "cause parties" that guests attend without having to also staff and host the cause party. The cause party can take on different forms: a clothing drive, a bake sale, a meet-and-greet with a local politician, a march or rally, a donation drive, a fundraiser, a public art project to raise awareness, a YouTube video to draw attention to a particular issue, a book breaking down big concepts, political pins for sale or giveaway to spread the word, a well-written petition. Your "guests" to the party can then donate clothes, buy a cookie, come by and listen to the politician's speech, show up as a marcher, donate money, look at an art piece and think about it, read the book, wear a pin, sign a petition. Basically, they show up, give money, agree to consume a piece of information you want them to know, or agree to take a certain specific, discrete action. The key difference between you-the-host and them-the-guests is that you are not expecting them to do the behind-the-scenes work of creating the pin, writing the book, figuring out exactly how and whom to give the money to, organizing a march route, etc. You are throwing the party and your gift to guests is that they can enjoy being a part of the cause without having to do the organizational work. Your cause benefits from you bringing more people to it.

And the final step is, when you're not too busy organizing your own cause parties, show up to other people's cause parties as a guest and an ally.

This isn't unlike being in high school, and joining the board of one or two clubs—say, the Spanish club and the debate team. These took a lot of time and effort to organize and keep things going, but you still had time to do your homework, be a kid, and go support your friends' groups, like being in the audience for football games, mathlete competitions, etc.

For the Pussyhat Project, a group of four motivated women busted their asses for six days to launch the Pussyhat Project manifesto, the website, and all the social media handles. We were the party hosts. This allowed thousands of women to attend as "guests" by knitting hats or wearing them. And hundreds of impassioned women decided to promote themselves from guest to cohost by hosting knit nights, making a YouTube how-to-knit video, knitting pussyhats for public statues, and otherwise figuring out ways to bring more people to the cause.

So go throw a party and change the world.

Conclusion: The State of Duh

# CONCLUSION
# The State of Duh

## Dear Reader,

It is my hope that this book has given you the tools and talismans that will aid you to speak up in this WTF world.

I wish that these tools were unnecessary. I personally describe the goal of feminism as "the State of Duh," a world where the idea that a woman deserves equality, safety, and self-expression is noncontroversial. When we are in a place where we no longer have to fight for those ideas, when they are instead accepted as "of course, duh," then feminism has won.

As much as I have loved writing this book, it is my dearest wish that one day *DIY Rules for a WTF World* becomes irrelevant. In the meantime, I hope you and every other woman learns to listen to her intuition, to fight for her voice, and to recognize that our issues are not frivolous. I yearn for the day we can clink glasses because we achieved the State of Duh. Until we get there, I want to thank you for being a part of the movement.

In a commencement speech to Bryn Mawr's graduating class, Ursula K. Le Guin said, "When women speak truly they speak subversively—they can't help it: if you're underneath, if you're kept down, you break out, you subvert. We are volcanoes. When we women offer our experience as our truth, as human truth, all the maps change. There are new mountains. That's what I want—to hear you erupting. You young Mount St. Helenses who don't know the power in you—I want to hear you."

The personal is political.

The personal is subversive.

Erupt. Speak out. The world needs you to.

I am sending you much love.

# Acknowledgments

Every screenwriter in Hollywood has a draft. I'm not talking about a draft of a screenplay, I'm talking about the draft of her OSCAR SPEECH. Personally, I would edit mine every month, adding people who helped me, taking off people who wronged me. It was a vindictive thrill.

The acknowledgments of this book, however, come from a much more wholesome place in my heart.

I want to thank all the feminist warriors who came before me and who support me now, some in my blood family, some who are unrelated but who are my sisters in thought and purpose. Thank you for all you do, seen and unseen. I am so grateful to you.

And before I go on to my list of people I'd like to spotlight, I want you to know how much I love and thank *you*, Reader of This Book, for opening your mind and heart to my ideas, and I hope you go on to treat your ideas with the same respect, openness, and joy that you've treated mine. I so look forward to what you make. Thank you for reading, for speaking up, for reveling in your own creativity, and for changing the world.

Here are some of the many many people I am grateful for:

My family! Mom, Dad, my Pwo Pwo and Grandma who taught me how to knit, my Gong Gong and Grandpa, my brothers Matt and Jeff, my aunts and uncles and cousins—with particular thanks to Aunt Celia and Aunt Kathy for knitting so many pussyhats. You've raised me, believed in me, challenged me, and have always wanted the best for me, including a better, safer world for me to live in. Because of you, I want to be part of creating that better, safer world for all of us. Thank you so much.

## XOXOXOXOXOX

My Pussyhat family: Kat Coyle and the army of knitters, crocheters, Ravelry witches, LYS community builders, yarn-bombers, and super caring people like you who made the project possible to exist and impossible to ignore.

Kat Coyle—when I texted you that day, I was brimming over with excitement. Thank you for always being so supportive of my ideas and helping me make them real—I wanted to make a flowered blanket having never crocheted in the round and you helped me; I wanted to make a Sea of Pink having never written a pattern and you helped me. You don't see obstacles, only opportunities to learn, teach, and create—you really are a national treasure.

Jayna Zweiman—my crochet buddy who became my cofounder of the Pussyhat Project—you grokked your genius, and from the beginning saw the vision as nothing less than huge. Together we foretold yarn shortages, *New Yorker* covers, museum exhibits, and made them real. We never caved in to the pressure to think small, which in itself is such a feminist achievement. I feel so lucky to have had the right person at the right time jump on board this amazing ride just as we set off.

Aurora Lady—my artist divine, I am so glad I met you before the Pussyhat Project and that we had just enough of a connection for me to ask you to pull off the impossible: Can you draw the cover of the Pussyhat Project manifesto? In four days? And maybe also the interior . . . and maybe also the back cover . . . and maybe also handle the Instagram launch? I love the punk artist girl-pop sensibility you have in your art and in your life. It continually inspires me, and I love that the Pussyhat Project was only the beginning—together we have created art for my website, maps of my favorite places, love letters, and the artwork for this book. The joy of working with you is not only in the beautiful results but in the gorgeous process—you've shown me that communication in collaboration is such an exquisite art form. Your philosophy as an artist has inspired me to keep moving forward. And your art is perfect.

The McKnight family (Carrie, Claudia, Molly, Evan, and Emily), Liz Leong, Stefanie Kamerman, Alexandra Arnhold, and Code Pink—there is so much work you did, but I want to particularly thank you for that week in D.C. before the march. I will never forget how beautiful it was to be united in purpose with such amazing, kind, and capable human beings.

## XOXOXOXOXOX

My family of creatives, mentors, and friends, and of course, my "book family."

Nancy Conyers, Libby Costin, and Lisa Feintech—Nancy would want me to point out that of you three I've known Nancy the longest! Thank you so much for believing in me from moment one, and holding that belief for me when my own confidence faltered. Thank you for showing me Sweden, for being ballers, and for being the first to donate to the Pussyhat Project!

Alissa Davis—thank you for sharing and letting me share our yucky beautiful truths—in the car, at the bar, on the beach. I feel blessed and #blessed to get to connect with you in this lifetime. I love your magic.

Yumi Sakugawa—from the corridors of Troy to the deserts of Santa Fe, thank you for being my friend and for "grokking me" and for exploring new territories of self-improvement and adventure with me. Thank you for being the unique starseed you are.

MILCK—Connie, you are so *gene*. I'm so grateful we created a space where ideas like the Pussyhat Project and the I Can't Keep Quiet movement can flourish. You are one of the most nurturing badass women I know.

Emily Rapp—you are such a superstar. I love the breakthroughs that happened with this book while I was in Palm Springs with you eating burritos. Thank you for showing me that true champions exist.

Geneva Burleigh—you kept your sense of humor even when I was at my worst. Thank you for braving traffic and conquering parking to meet in Larchmont Village.

Thank you, Grand Central Publishing, in particular:

Gretchen Young—I had such a good feeling about you when I first met you, and my intuition was right!

Katherine Stopa—I am so grateful that you had sincere appreciation of the book while being a careful editor—thank you!

Kamrun Nesa and Tiffany Sanchez—the energy you bring to this book is so appreciated.

Thank you to whoever made the decision to make this book FULL COLOR! I am so in awe of you for making this bold (entirely correct) decision! Thank you to the whole team at GCP for believing in this book.

Thank you to my agent Sara Crowe, and Leila Howland for introducing me to her, and Jon Davis for introducing me to Leila. I treasure my relationships with each and every one of you.

And thank you Akello Stone (my big brother), Alyssa Lazo, Breelyn Burns, Rachael Lee Stroud, Kelly Cree, Jessica Mullen, Dan O'Shannon, Lauren Russo, and Gwynnie Bran Hale for helping with everything under the sun. And thank you Huong Ngo and Jack Daniel (the man, not the drink) for making time to listen to me between the Pussyhat Project idea conception and the march—having you two available to hold space for me was invaluable.

To be continued at the Oscars . . .

XOXO
Krista

P.S. Thank YOU, yes YOU, again!

SARA CROWE

ALISSA DAVIS

Kat Coyle

The McKnight Family
(Carrie, Claudia, Molly, Evan and Emily)

Gretchen Young

Emily Rapp

GWYNNIE BRAN HALE

AKELLO STONE

ALYSSA LAZO

KAMRUN NESA

Thank you

LIZ LEONG

LEILA HOWLAND

JACK    DANIEL

RACHAEL LEE STROUD

TIFFANY SANCHEZ

GENEVA BURLEIGH

M&L CK

Yumi Sakagawa

Aurora Lady

NANCY CONYERS

LIBBY COSTIN

LISA FEINTECH

Dan O'Shannon

KELLY CREE    JESSICA MULLIN

HUONG NGO

Jayna Zweiman

Katherine Stopa

My Family

Grand Central Publishing

LAUREN RUSSO

ALEX ARNHOLD

Stephanie Kamerman

JON DAVIS

We all know what happened on November 8, 2016 👖💀

Nov. 12, 2016
Krista dreams up: ▱!
She texts Kat immediately.

Nov. 18, 2016
Aurora comes on board to illustrate!

pussyhatproject.com

Nov. 22, 2016
The Pussyhat website is launched, with manifesto and pattern.

Our volunteer family led by Molly McKnight in Reston, VA. collect over 12K hats to distribute at the Women's March on D.C. 173 allied knitstores across the country (and even a few international sites) collect even more hats. Knitters also give the hats directly to marchers headed to D.C. . . .

Amy Schumer    Patti Smith

Crafters, activists, celebrities, etc. start to get on board. People all over the country were knitting away. We caused a run on pink yarn!

Nov. 16, 2016
Krista and Jayna gather at Kat's store:
THE LITTLE KNITTERY ♡
Kat begins the pattern. What follows
is 6 days of hard work.

Nov. 17, 2016
Kat's first 🎩 comes off the needles.
Krista and Jayna witness this moment.

Nov. 23 (the day before Thanksgiving)
Launched social media campaign
on Instagram + Facebook

More volunteers like Molly, Stefanie,
and Liz join this massive
movement! Lending skills like
community organizing, photography,
and PR!

Timeline
of the
Pussyhat
Project

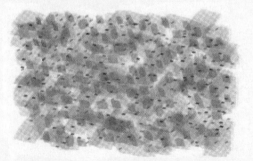

And on January 21, 2017 we created a huge
"flag of resistance" for the world to see ♡

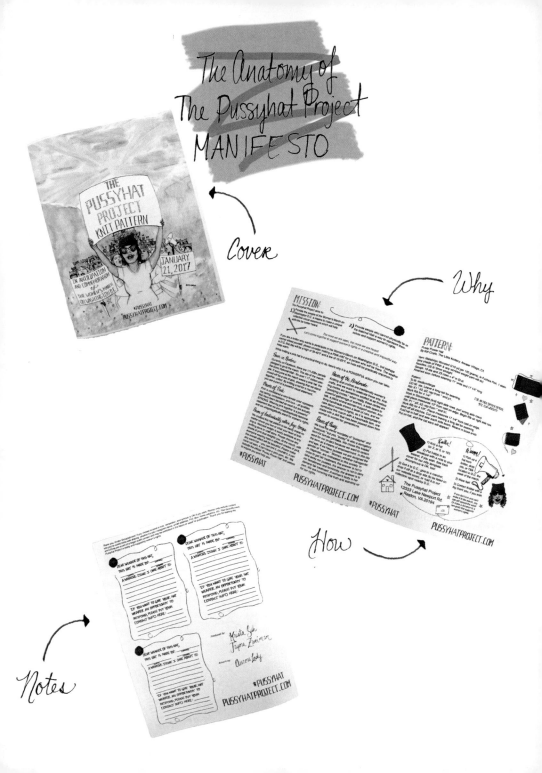

The Anatomy of
The Pussyhat Project
MANIFESTO

Cover

Why

How

Notes

# Pussyhat Knit Pattern

Included here is the original pussyhat pattern, created in anticipation and commemoration of the Women's March on January 21, 2017.

Gathered together, people wearing the pussyhat can recreate the sea of pink, a powerful statement that we are here and that we stand together, strong.

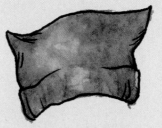

## The Pussy Power Hat Pattern by Kat Coyle

**Yarn:** Malabrigo Worsted (100% Kettle Dyed Pure Merino Wool; 210 yd per 100 g) in 093 Fuchsia, 1 skein (any shade of PINK and any brand of worsted weight yarn will do)

**Needles:** US 8/5 mm straight

**Gauge:** 18 sts and 23 rows = 4" in St st

**Finished Size:** before seaming 11" wide and 17¼" long

### Pattern

**To fit:** medium/large

CO 50 sts. Leave a long tail for seaming.

Rib: K1 * k2, p2; rep from * end p1.

Work rib for 4¼".

Work in Stockinette st (knit right side rows, purl wrong side rows) until piece measures 13" from cast-on edge.

Rib: P1 * p2, k2; rep from * end k1.

Work rib for 4¼". Piece measures 17¼" from cast-on edge.

Bind off all stitches. Cut yarn, leaving a long tail for seaming.

Fold hat in half and sew each side seam. Weave in loose ends.

Put on hat, and the cat ears will appear!

# Evil Eye Glove Knit Pattern

In anticipation of the midterm elections on November 6, 2018, here is a sneak peek into my next craftivist project: the Evil Eye Glove. Making, giving, and wearing these gloves makes me feel so loved, protected, and powerful. If we gather in a crowd together, wearing these gloves, we can create a sea of eyes to show that the people are watching. To show we are vigilant and we take care of each other. Let's make the midterm elections a turning point in history. For more information, please see kristasuh.com

## The Evil Eye Glove Pattern by Kat Coyle

**Yarn:** Malabrigo Worsted (100% Kettle Dyed Pure Merino Wool; 210 yd per 100g)

**MC:** 036 Pearl, 1 skein

**CC:** 196 Black, a few yards for embroidering the outline of the eye

**CC1:** 150 Azul Profundo, a few yards for embroidering the iris

**CC2:** a few yards of white worsted weight wool for embroidering and weaving in ends

**Needles:** US 8/5 mm straight

**Notions:** tapestry needle for sewing seam, embroidery, and weaving in ends

**Gauge:** 18 sts and 26 rows = 4" in St st

**Finished Size:** Hand 6 (7, 8)" circ and 7¾" long

*Note: Glove is knit flat from wrist to hand.*

## Pattern

Make two (shown in 6" circ size).

With US 8 needle and MC, CO 28 (32, 36) sts.

Leave a long tail for seaming.

Knit 6 rows.

Work in Stockinette st (knit right side rows, purl wrong side rows) until piece measures 7½" from cast on edge.

Knit 6 rows.

BO all sts.

## Finishing

Begin at cast-on edge. Use the long tail and tapestry needle to sew seam (about 3½") to thumb opening. Leave 2" space for thumb, resume sewing seam to top of glove. Neatly weave in loose ends.

## Embroidery

With Black yarn, embroider the outline of the eye and eyelashes using stem stitch. First establish the shape of the eye and then proceed to the eyelashes. With Blue, embroider the iris of the eye using a type of blanket stitch that forms a circle.

The white of the eye is embroidered using the duplicate stitch.

# Suggested Resources

**People**

    Lauren Russo, life coach (www.laurendrusso.com)

    Gwynnie Bran Hale, herbalist (www.gwynniebird.com)

**Nonfiction**

    *The Artist's Way* by Julia Cameron

    *The Big Leap* by Gay Hendricks

    *The Fire Starter Sessions* by Danielle LaPorte

    *The Five Love Languages* by Gary Chapman

    *God, Help Me Tie My Shoes!* by Anthony Goulet

    *Mama Gena's School of Womanly Arts* by Regena Thomashauer

    *Mirror Work* by Louise Hay

    *Outrageous Openness* by Tosha Silver

    *Women, Food, and God* by Geneen Roth

    *Your Illustrated Guide to Becoming One with the Universe* by
        Yumi Sakugawa

**Fiction**

These are books I think you'll enjoy and that inspire me, sometimes in indirect ways.

    *The Big Love* by Sarah Dunn

    *Dietland* by Sarai Walker

    *Graceling* by Kristin Cashore

    The Grisha Trilogy by Leigh Bardugo

**Podcast**

    Brooke Castillo's Life Coach School, episode 12: "Boundaries" (https://
        thelifecoachschool.com/12/)

### Online Articles and Videos

"The Work" by Byron Katie (http://thework.com/en/do-work)

"I'm Not Living Up to My Full Potential" by Byron Katie (YouTube) (https://www.youtube.com/watch?v=GM4jtnR6pww)

"My Mother Shamed Me" by Byron Katie (YouTube) (https://www.youtube.com/watch?v=q71APV6LUjI)

"What I Learned from 100 Days of Rejection" by Jia Jiang (TEDTalk) (https://www.ted.com/talks/jia_jiang_what_i_learned_from_100_days_of_rejection)

### Courses

INFLUENCE by Carolyn Grace Elliott (http://carolyngraceelliott.com/)

Big Breakthrough Weekend by Alejandra Crisafulli (http://www.coachwithalejandra.com/)

B-School by Marie Forleo (https://www.marieforleo.com/bschool/)

### Personality Tests

Myers-Briggs

StrengthsFinder 2.0

Five Love Languages

How to Fascinate

Enneagram

### Songs

"You Got It" by Roy Orbison

"(I Can't Keep) Quiet" by MILCK

"Everybody Plays the Fool" by The Main Ingredient

"Turn Turn Turn" by The Byrds

"Ring of Keys" from the musical *Fun Home*

### Meditation Resources

Stop, Breathe, Think app by Mind Body Awareness

Oprah and Deepak's 21-Day Meditation Experience